Creative Slide/Tape Programs

Creative Slide/Tape Programs

Lee Green

1986

Libraries Unlimited   **Littleton, Colorado**

LIBRARIES UNLIMITED, INC.
P.O. Box 263
Littleton, Colorado 80160-0263

Users of this book are advised to take the provisions of Public Law 94-553 (the U.S. Copyright Law) into account in all projects they may undertake in creating slide/tape programs. Neither the author nor the publisher of this book intend to suggest exceptions to that law.

Library of Congress Cataloging-in-Publication Data

Green, Lee.
    Creative slide/tape programs.

    Bibliography: p. 133
    1. Media programs (Education)--Planning. 2. Slides (Photography)--Planning. 3. Transparencies in education-- Planning. 4. Phonotapes in education--Planning.
I. Title.
LB1028.4.G74   1986   371.3'35   86-10462
ISBN 0-87287-444-3

Libraries Unlimited books are bound with Type II nonwoven material that meets and exceeds National Association of State Textbook Administrators' Type II nonwoven material specifications Class A through E.

Table of Contents

Acknowledgments

The preparation of a book requires ideas and assistance from others. I am fortunate to have had the creative talents of Mark Hendrickson, from whom I have learned many things about hand lettering and quick graphic production. To Jerry Burgess, with his wide photographic background, a big thank-you for taking, developing, and printing the photographs in this book.

I thank my wife, Pat, for putting up with books and papers scattered around the house.

Introduction

Most books written on slide/tape production are written for professional producers and deal with production techniques far beyond the capability of the amateur. This book is written specifically for teachers and students, library/media specialists, leaders of service organizations, and business people who often have a limited amount of production expertise, time, money, or equipment. I have elected to write on slide/tape production because I firmly believe that this medium is the most powerful and versatile available to the amateur producer. *It is both inexpensive and easy to produce.* Slides can give much the same impact as 16mm and video at a fraction of the cost. And, with a few hours of training in planning procedures, and the use of automatic cameras, anyone can produce good, useable slide/tape programs. *Slide/tape offers flexibility.* Slides can be easily rearranged, and updated. Programs may be targeted to the needs and backgrounds of specific age groups from kindergarten to senior citizens. *Slide/tape programs hold audience attention.* Not everyone is an accomplished communicator, but anyone can be more effective using visuals to present a message. You can also say more in a carefully planned 15-minute slide/tape program than in a 15-minute oral talk. Besides, television and films have conditioned the public to expect graphic and visual presentation of ideas. Furthermore, research has shown that we remember what we see longer than we remember what we only hear. Due to the nature of the medium, *slide/tape programs provide vicarious experience.* You can bring the sight and sound of Asia, Africa, or South America into the room. They also allow the sharing of cross-cultural experiences. *Slide/tape programs can change attitudes.* TV commercials are a testimonial to the power of visualization. I have seen slide/tape programs have the same effect. *Slide/tape can set a mood.* Slide/tape programs are more emotionally than intellectually based. They can create an aura, they can move people. Two or more media working together produce a greater effect than the same media used independently. There is a synergism; beautiful photography, sound effects, music, and a well-written script enhance each other.

Good slide/tape programs have many uses in the school. They enable you to:

- Present overviews of instructional programs.

- Introduce the subject or main ideas in a unit of study.

- Teach a specific skill.

- Motivate otherwise disinterested students.

- Provide orientation to facilities such as the library/media center.

- Provide orientation before a field trip.

- Give students ideas for projects in art or in science.

- Allow students to illustrate stories they have written or produce photo essays.

- Record special events such as field days.

- Inform parents of classroom activities during back-to-school night.

- Play back the highlights of the school year.

This is a medium with which children can become involved. A wide range of writing and communication skills can be developed through slide/tape production.

For those reading this book who are not involved in education, the slide/tape program is the least expensive locally produced audiovisual tool for promoting an idea, product, or process. I recently assisted the owners of a newly formed company to produce a presentation designed to teach sales representatives about their line of cosmetics, but there are many other possibilities. You might:

- Present an overview of the structure of your organization.

- Explore key social issues relevant to the community.

- Give step-by-step instructions.

- Show highlights of a visit made to a foreign country or to a state or national park.

- Present the history of your own community.

In the back of this book are more than 200 ideas for slide/tape programs.

Much time and money can be saved if we know how to plan a slide/tape program systematically from the initial idea to the finished product. This book will explain step-by-step, as simply as possible, how to take an idea and plan a program that will be professional and will communicate the desired message. Technology has produced camera equipment that is fully automatic even to the focusing of the picture. Most of us have some type of audio equipment. Thus, you probably already have the equipment needed to produce quality slide/tape programs.

We are now ready to begin the step-by-step planning process of a slide/tape program. It is best that you have a topic in mind as you go through the actual planning process. To learn these skills you must become involved in using them. If you don't have a topic, look in the back of this book for ideas. Now let us begin.

1
How to
Start Planning

TOPIC SELECTION

Often students, teachers, or organizations want to begin the process of making a slide/tape program by shooting slides. This may be appropriate when you are taking a trip to another country and do not know what to expect, and it is therefore difficult to plan a script. Generally, however, there is no substitute for careful planning before the slides are taken to make instructional slide/tape programs effective and inexpensive.

Perhaps the most difficult part of the planning process for beginners is selecting a narrow topic. Sometimes after you have worked on a slide/tape program for a while, you find that you have taken on more than you can present in a single program. It is much less discouraging to start with a narrow topic than to have to scrap a script and begin again. The main question is, "How do I know if the topic I have selected is too broad?"

A good way to determine the answer is to write a brief treatment of your presentation in a paragraph or two. If you cannot cover the key ideas of your program in a couple of brief paragraphs then you should think about narrowing your topic. Try to focus on a single idea or theme in your presentation. Beginners generally choose topics that are too broad and complex. So beware. At first the topic may seem too simple or narrow, but this seldom turns out to be the case.

One Idea

AUDIENCE ANALYSIS

Audience analysis is interwoven with the formation of objectives, discussed below. To be effective you must know who your audience will be. You must know what they know about the subject and their attitude toward the subject, and you must determine the pace at which you will present the information. A teacher or library/media specialist should be very familiar with the background of the students who will view the presentation. In cases where the target audience is not well known you may want to find the answers to some of the following questions:

What does the audience know about the subject?

What do the audience members know about the subject?

What are their ages?

What is their educational background?

What is their socioeconomic level?

What are their occupations?

What biases do they have and what is their attitude about the topic?

Why am I presenting the program and why are they watching the program?

What is their interest in the subject?

What types of visuals or background music might be offensive to them?

These are important questions. The more you understand your audience the greater potential for the success of your slide/tape program.

BEHAVIORAL OBJECTIVES

Objectives should be written with the behavior of the audience in mind. What behavioral changes do you want to result from your presentation? Do you want to change the audience's attitude? Do you want to motivate its members to do something? Do they need to learn certain skills?

What behavioral changes do you want?

Good objectives should

1. be stated in terms of learner behavior

2. describe an observable performance or product

3. state the condition of performance

4. state the standard of performance

Many of the words often used to write objectives are vague and open to different interpretations—for example, *understand* and *appreciate*. If you write slide/tape program objectives in vague terms you will not be able to evaluate the program's success. Thus the statement which communicates best is the one which describes the terminal behavior of the viewer well enough to preclude misinterpretation. Here are some examples of vague terms used in objective writing:

to know	to understand	to really understand
to appreciate	to fully appreciate	to have faith in
to enjoy	to believe	to grasp the significance of

Use measureable verbs

Here are a few examples of verbs which give more precision to objective writing:

build	classify	compose
define	describe	explain
label	match	prepare
recognize	list	compare
construct	identify	differentiate
use the equivalent of	arrange from left to right	name from youngest to oldest

(See appendix A for a fuller list.)

Useful statements of objectives are made up of two grammatical parts: first, a specific action verb like those in the illustrations above; second, a content reference that follows the verb—for example, "name *five steps in a process*"; "apply *a rule*." The following examples contrast an ambiguous with a specific objective.

Ambiguous: To know how the local water supply is treated.

Specific: To be able to name the five steps in the purification process of our local water supply.

When producing a slide/tape program, it is a good idea to write your objectives on a 3 x 5 card and keep them before you throughout the planning and scripting process. To help you in topic selection, audience analysis, and objective writing, a planning worksheet is included in appendix B. Use this to begin your planning process.

OUTLINE DEVELOPMENT

Once you have determined your topic, analyzed your audience, and written the objectives, the next step is to develop an outline of your presentation. A simple way to do this is to take a piece of scratch paper and at the top jot down your topic. For example, let's say that you are going to present "How to Interview for a Job." Begin brainstorming all the possible ideas pertaining to your topic. Write these down, using a few words or short phrases for each. Do not seek to evaluate these ideas at this time. When you have "run dry," let the ideas sit for a while. Later, return to your sheet of ideas and begin evaluating them. You will find some are good and some rather pathetic. Cross out the bad ideas. Place a star by the four or five key ideas. Try to select those ideas that seem to fit together, and omit the rest.

Brainstorm all possible ideas pertaining to your topic

Next, number your ideas in what seems to be the best order of presentation. Remember, planning at this point is still preliminary, and ideas may be changed or rearranged. On another sheet of paper write out these ideas in the order they are going to be presented. Leave room after each idea for subpoints, and flesh out your outline by filling in the subpoints under each main idea.

LEADING INTO YOUR PRESENTATION

The next thing you must decide is how you are going to lead your audience into your subject. In the first 30 seconds of your program your viewers will either become interested in your subject or turned off and perhaps tune you out.

First thirty seconds most important

There are several ways to create interest at the beginning of a slide/tape program. Sound effects such as a crying baby or a chugging locomotive will immediately gain the attention of the audience. A series of close-up shots of interesting people without commentary can be used to lead into your subject and hold interest. Lively lead-in music also is a help in grabbing an audience. An aura of mystery may be created by using a series of close-ups such as a hand on a doorknob or feet walking or shadowy figures. The best way to get creative ideas is to view motion pictures or television and analyze how the writers led into the program. Select something that you think you could do, but be realistic about your capabilities.

EVALUATION

Once you have completed your outline and have decided how you are going to lead into your program you are a long way into the successful production of a slide/tape program. Now is a good time to present your ideas to a sympathetic friend or colleague and ask for suggestions. Don't be defensive, but listen carefully to their evaluation.

Ask yourself again if your presentation is simple, with one main idea or theme. Do you have too much material for one presentation? Do the main points of your outline have continuity? Have you considered your objectives in developing your outline? Considering your budget and resources, can this program realistically be produced?

Review your outline once more, and then sit back and close your eyes. Go through your presentation mentally, visualizing it as you want the audience to see it. You must think visually rather than logically. Remember that at least 80 percent of your presentation will be told by visuals. You will have a two-column script, on the left a description of the visual, and on the right, the audio. In a good presentation, words and images will be closely related. So let your mind's eye go to work to develop images to tell your story. This is good preparation for your upcoming decision about what kinds of photographs and graphics to use. First, however, you have more organizational work to do. Once you have mentally gone through your presentation you must put it down on paper in the form of a storyboard or production script.

2
How to Develop Storyboard Cards or a Production Script

Storyboarding is the procedure for organizing a sequence of visuals and narration to tell a story or present information. There are two ways of storyboarding—using 4 x 6 cards or using a production script. Each has its advantages and disadvantages.

When 4 x 6 cards are used, each card represents one slide and the narration about that slide. Cards give a great deal of flexibility because their sequence can easily be changed and cards can easily be added or deleted.

Title	Frame No
	Notes:
Narration:	

Storyboard card.

A production script consists of a page or pages with a column of rectangles, each representing a slide, on the left side, and space on the right side for the narration (see appendix A). The advantage of a production script is that you can more easily see the continuity in what you are planning. Furthermore, a slide/tape program may be planned completely on a production script, thus saving time. The production script is handy if you are adapting the narration from another source which is already written, such as a pamphlet; if you are matching slides with music, without narration; or if you have a detailed outline to follow. The main disadvantage of the script is the lack of flexibility that cards give. It is inconvenient to add or delete slides or rearrange their sequence.

Generally storyboard cards or production scripts should be numbered and dated and include the name of the program, a description of each slide, slide numbers, camera angle, and narration. When storyboarding, use a soft lead pencil so that changes may be made. The planning process at this time should remain very fluid. If 4 x 6 cards are used, upon completion of the planning process they may be laid out on a table or tacked to a bulletin board to be studied and analyzed. The cards then may be rearranged and renumbered if necessary. Once the pencil version of the production script is completed, the pages may be typed in a more final form. This then becomes the reading script (see appendix A). This script will help anyone producing the audio part of your program. It will be readily understood by a radio announcer or sound studio technicians. It may later be used as a guide for anyone presenting your slide program. A reading script is especially necessary if you do not program or place beeps on your sound track.

COMBINING IMAGE AND NARRATIVE

We have already talked about the process of visualizing what you are saying in your script. To be most effective the slide and narrative must mesh: the narrative must complement and enhance the image. It need not, however, be lengthy. Choose your words carefully—think of them as costing 25 cents each. Sometimes a single phrase or word is all that is needed to accompany a specific slide. Sometimes you may want to suspend the narration and show a slide or a sequence in silence, or replace the narration with music. Narration can get in the way of a slide that has strong visual impact. Whatever your decision about the image-and-narrative combination, avoid describing the image the audience will be seeing on the screen.

WRITING THE NARRATIVE

Whether you use storyboard cards or a production script, keep your objective card before you as you write. Because slide/tape programs are so versatile, there is no set way to plan a storyboard. Sometimes, you may write out the complete narration first and then select or plan slides to illustrate your ideas. The weakness of this method is that you may insert slides that do not illustrate the concepts in your script to best advantage. The author has seen many professionally produced filmstrips and slide/tape programs in which it was difficult to follow the narration because the visuals were not related to the script. A better method is to mentally visualize the content of your program in sequences of visuals. The audio should be an adjunct to the visuals, not the reverse. Use words to fill in gaps and background information not visualized. This will better blend the narration with the visuals.

A conversational tone for the narrative works best. Achieving such a tone is more difficult for some writers than others. To check your success, read the storyboard out loud or have someone read it to you. It should sound as though you are talking to the audience rather than reading from a book. Here is a tip for writing in a conversational tone. Sit at a table and imagine you are facing a friend and drinking a soft drink as you tape record your conversation. You might

begin by saying, "I just came up with this great idea." You may want to talk through your idea several times, recording, then listening, evaluating, and revising. It may take a while to get over the surprise of hearing your own voice. Another technique is to imagine that you are writing a letter to a friend. Tell him or her the same things you talked about on the tape recorder. Use the same casual, conversational style you used on your tape recording. You may use incomplete sentences or phrases, as we often do in conversation. In conversation we also use many contractions—I'm, can't, didn't. Think in terms of rather short, simple sentences. On the other hand, don't be too simplistic; try to write the way you would talk to a friend.

USING INTERVIEWS

It may be difficult to script for an interview. It may be enough just to write out the questions you will ask and give them ahead of time to the person to be interviewed. The interviewee may make notes to use in answering. The author has sometimes written out a script for the interviewee so that the information needed will be sure to be included. However, some people cannot read a script so that it sounds natural. A 3 x 5 card with an outline of the interview also may be used so everyone knows the direction the interview will go. Do not spring any surprises on your interviewee. Ask him or her to answer as concisely as possible. Editing interview material is a very time-consuming task.

PACING THE PROGRAM

Pace is most important in slide/tape production. If the pace is too fast it will leave the audience confused and panting. Too fast a pace will also not allow you time to synchronize the slides and the audio with a cassette tape recorder/programmer. A wordy or slow-paced program will bore the audience unless there is high interest in the subject.

Slow pace is boring

It is most important to remember that audiences have developed a certain sophistication concerning visual presentations through watching films and television. They are used to fast-moving programs. The average TV shot is on the screen seven seconds. Programs that you plan may not have that fast a pace, but they should not drag and bore the audience.

The average shot on TV lasts seven seconds.

Pace is expressed by the number of slides presented per minute.

Pace = Number of slides per minute

Let us assume that you are going to use a Kodak Carousel projector and either a 80- or 140-slide tray. Let us also assume that you are going to present a new slide on the average of every 7 seconds. (This means that some slides may be on the screen 2 seconds, and others, 15. The pace *should* vary.) If a slide remains on the screen for more than 20 seconds it must have high visual impact or the audience will become bored.

No more than 20 seconds on the screen

Assuming that you show a new slide on the average of every 7 seconds, the pace of your presentation is approximately 8½ slides per minute (60 seconds divided by 7 equals 8 +). If you are using an 80-slide tray and showing 8 + slides per minute you would have about 9½

A new slide every seven seconds

minutes to present the program (80 divided by 8.5 equals 9 +). If you use a 140-slide tray you would have about a 16½-minute program (140 divided by 8.5 equals 16 +). You could of course have longer programs by using more than one slide tray. You could also have two projectors and a dissolve unit for longer programs. However, for classroom use it is better to stay with a single-tray presentation. It is also a good idea to keep programs under 20 minutes in length. Obviously, the narration you write for each slide must be succinct.

Keep programs under 20 minutes

DECIDING ON TYPES OF SHOTS

Concerning the use of images (as opposed to graphics) in slide/tape programs, it is wise to vary the angle and type of shot so that you have a series of slides that really tell the story, rather than a series of snapshots. To help you decide on the type of shot most effective for a given situation, here are descriptions of various types of shots. Their abbreviations are useful when the angle of the shot is noted on the reading script (see appendix A).

Long shot (LS) or establishment shot (ES): A shot that orients the audience to the scene of the action; it relates the subject to the background.

Medium shot (MS): A shot featuring the subject, with the background being only incidental.

Close-up shot (CU): A shot calling attention to part of the subject, such as a facial expression or a clenched fist.

Extreme close-up shot (ECU): This is a strong emphasis shot in which the lips, a ring finger, or an eye may fill the screen.

Long shot.

Medium shot.

Close-up shot.

Extreme close-up.

High-angle shot (HA): A shot taken with the camera looking down on the subject. This diminishes the importance of the subject.

High-angle shot.

Low-angle shot (LA): A shot made with the camera looking up at the subject. This gives the subject an aura of dominance.

Low-angle shot.

There are a number of other shots such as medium close-up, medium long, over-the-shoulder, and montage. A montage is a series of brief shots shown in quick succession to create an emotional effect. It may condense weeks or months of action into a brief moment.

GUIDELINES FOR PRODUCTION SCRIPTING

Here are fourteen guidelines for production scripting that have been found useful.

1. Remember this is an audiovisual presentation. Try to imagine each visual as you write. Remember that 80 percent of your message will be carried by the visual.

80% of message carried by the visual!

2. Inside the rectangle on the storyboard card, write out a description of each slide or make pencil sketches using stick figures. You may want to go through your story and plan all or a sequence of visuals before writing the narrative. You may start your program with a focus slide, then a blank. Thus you may turn on your projector to start the program and have a blank screen. When the audio starts your first slide appears on the screen. Thus you begin the written part of your program with slide number three on the tray.

3. Each storyboard card should include, along with a description of the slide, the slide number, camera angle (close-up, long shot, high angle, etc.), and the narration.

6 INCHES

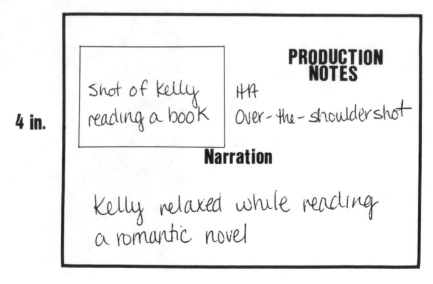

4 in.

Shot of Kelly reading a book

HA
Over-the-shoulder shot

PRODUCTION NOTES

Narration

Kelly relaxed while reading a romantic novel

4. Regarding the narration, write in a conversational tone. As stated before, the tone can be tested by having someone read the script to you aloud, or by recording it on tape and listening to it. Have a friend listen to it and give constructive criticism. Do this three or four times at least on your first production.

5 . Choose words carefully, and use them sparingly. Think of them as costing 25 cents each. Sometimes a phrase or a single word is all that is needed for a particular slide, or you may not need to say anything. A strong image can carry the message alone.

> # Word = 25¢

6. When writing in conversational tone, you may break the rules of grammar if your presentation demands it. For example, if a character in your program is a tough old miner, use the type of language he would use. You may want to use a dramatic type of script, using several voices rather than a narrator. Interview-type scripts are also interesting. Using more than one voice in a script adds interest.

7. Use colorful action words. However, beware of overused adjectives. Use a dictionary or *Roget's Thesaurus* to find synonyms. Try not to repeat the same word within one sentence unless for special emphasis. Avoid alliteration—too many words beginning with the same letter in a sentence. These often form tongue twisters which are difficult for the narrator. (Reading scripts out loud will reveal a lot of these.) Don't use slang—it may be unfamiliar to the audience and it could become dated.

8. When using all but the most familiar abbreviations, explain what they stand for. For example, if you will be using "AMA" for the American Medical Association often during the program, define the abbreviation at its first occurence in the script.

> # Explain abbreviations

9. Remember that your audience cannot see the quotation marks on your script. Therefore, when using a quote, you must tell your audience. You may do this by saying, "and I quote" or "President Kennedy stated . . ." or "he spoke these words."

> # Tell the audience
> # when you quote

10. Do not describe what the audience sees on the screen. Use the narrative to add emphasis or give background information. For example, to accompany a shot of Mrs. Owens, the PTA president, the narrative could mention the office she holds — a fact not evident from viewing the slide.

11. Don't plan to have a slide on the screen for more than 15 to 20 seconds. The average TV shot is 7 seconds. Keep your program moving so that the audience isn't bored. Insert extra slides shot from a different perspective if you need to keep a subject on the screen for a longer time. Pace (how fast your program moves) will vary with the type of message presented and with the audience.

Keep program moving

12. Think in sequences of slides rather than individual shots. This may mean that you orient your audience to the action by using a long shot or medium shot and then move in for a series of close-up or extreme close-up shots. Generally, beginners do not take enough close-ups. Close-ups will tell your story and add interest. Analyze TV programs or motion pictures for their use of sequences to tell their stories. Note how many close-up shots they use.

Think in sequences of shots.

13. Vary the orientation of the shots you plan to use. Don't use shots taken exclusively at eye level. Shots of pets and children should be taken at their eye level, not yours. Over-the-shoulder shots show what a performer is doing from his point of view and are good for demonstrating "how-to" type skills. Use high- or low-angle shots to add variety.

Get shots of children from their eye level.

14. Plan your storyboard so well that you could give it to someone else to produce. Inadequate planning is the major weakness of beginning slide/tape producers.

EVALUATING THE STORYBOARD

After you have completed your storyboard, put it away for a day or two and let it age. When you return to it you will have what artists call a fresh eye. You will see the script differently. Read it into a tape recorder and play it back. Close your eyes and see if you can visualize your program as the storyboard is being presented. Do not be discouraged if it did not turn out exactly the way you wanted. REVISE. Remember, professional writers revise up to 8 or 10 times. Revising a script is not a sign of weakness, but rather part of being professional.

Ask a friend to consider the continuity (flow of events) of your program, and whether the proposed visuals carry the message. Is the narration too wordy? Does the pace of the program vary? Does it tend to drag, or is it too fast? Is the tone conversational? Do not argue with your friend's suggestions and criticisms. You don't have to accept them all, but think about them seriously. Another person may see ways to improve your program that you do not.

PLANNING THE VISUALS

Once you are satisfied that you have attained the best possible script, it is time to begin planning your visuals. Go through your storyboard cards or production script and make a list of all the slides needed for your slide/tape program. You should categorize each slide under one of the following headings (see appendix B):

Photographs to be taken indoors at each location

Photographs to be taken outdoors at each location

Graphic slides to be produced

Slides to be made using the copy stand (colored prints, drawings, magazine pictures; see chapter 6)

Photography and the production of graphic slides are discussed in detail in the chapters that follow.

3
Photography

Although this chapter is dedicated to photographic techniques, you need not be an experienced photographer to put together a slide/tape program. If you are not well versed in photography and some of your shots are difficult ones, don't be afraid to ask for help. You can usually find someone who is happy to assist you. In some cases a helper may shoot the whole program for you. If you have an important message, poor slides can kill it. Don't think you have to do everything yourself.

If you are planning to do your own photography, your shooting assignment sheet (see appendix B) will be a useful organizational tool as you begin. Remember, regardless of where specific images fit in the sequence of your slide/tape program, you are going to take all the shots you need from each location at the same time. If you have to travel a distance to take some of your shots, remember, film is cheaper than your time. Take several alternate shots of each subject listed on each storyboard card. This may save you from having to come back a second time to reshoot some of your slides. Having too many slides gives several choices for each shot in the script. Also, some shots cannot be posed or planned entirely, so shoot lots of film to get the results you want.

CHOOSING A CAMERA

Because slide/tape programs are so varied and versatile there are many factors to consider when photographing. If this is a production planned and photographed by students as a learning project, very simple pocket cameras (like the Kodak Instamatic) may be used. If you are recording events in the classroom and need a lot of candid shots, a fully automatic camera with auto focus works well. Such cameras have built-in flash and free you to compose the picture.

If budget is a problem, a high-quality but obsolete camera may be purchased for a few dollars. If you are a teacher, ask parents to donate a camera they aren't going to use and take a tax write-off. Many school library/media centers have cameras for loan to students and teachers.

Parents may donate a quality obsolete camera.

You may want to purchase your own new camera for school and personal use. Check with your tax consultant. Sometimes the cost of equipment used as a part of your vocation can be deducted from your taxes. If you don't know what type of camera will best serve you, consult someone at a local camera store. Sales personnel must keep up with the latest in camera technology and can help you get the right camera for your budget and purpose. You will pay slightly more than you would at a discount store, but full-service camera stores offer a number of services worth the extra cost, including information concerning flash units, close-up photography, lenses, and how to maintain your camera, as well as a wide range of literature (see bibliography). Kodak publishes books and pamphlets on all phases of photography. They are priced reasonably and are very helpful. If you are serious about photography, subscribe to a photo magazine. Magazines often publish surveys on what is new in cameras and the ones they recommend. New developments in film are also discussed.

Do not buy a camera from a high-pressure sales person. Unless you are very knowledgeable, don't buy from mail order firms listed in camera magazines. If you buy any camera, check to see that the warranty is a United States one. Some gray-market cameras are brought into the country with warranties not valid in this country.

SELECTING FILM

The choice of film is often a matter of personal preference. There are, however, some guidelines that should be followed. Three terms designate the type of film: chrome (slides), color (color prints), and pan (black-and-white prints). For slide/tape use, Kodachrome is still the standard of the industry. It photographs yellows and reds well and has high resolution. Its main drawback is that it must be processed by Kodak and therefore must be mailed to the lab. This takes time. Other films like Ektachrome and Fujichrome may be locally developed—often 6- to 24-hour service is offered. This can be important if there are deadlines to be met. These films reproduce greens and blues well. The colors on the film box tell you what colors each film highlights. It is a good idea to try several different films and select the one you feel works best for you. Ektachrome and Fujichrome are now very fast films, allowing the use of available light in dimly lit situations.

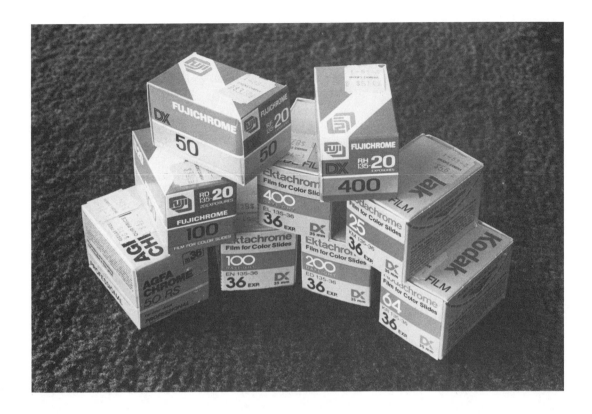

Chrome films.

If budget is a problem, outdated film is sometimes available at camera and discount stores at special prices. Sometimes merchants will donate film if they know it will be used by students for educational purposes. Don't be afraid to ask.

The speed printed on the box indicates the film's relative sensitivity to light. In the past film speed was expressed as ASA (United States) or DIN (Europe). It is now expressed as ISO and the speed number. The higher the number the more sensitive or faster the film. A fast film such as ISO 400 requires less light for exposure but will be more "grainy" than slower film. Let's use a simple illustration to explain film speed. Let's say you dig two post holes. In one you place two-inch washed rock; in the other, fine silt. Now, pour water into the holes. The hole with the rock will absorb the water quickly and the one with the silt slowly. Film is coated with silver crystals. Fast films have larger crystals and will absorb light faster, but the larger crystals will show up as grain and thus the image will be less distinct when projected. Slower films such as Kodachrome 64 or Fujichrome 100 will give sharp pictures with little grain. If you are shooting under difficult lighting conditions, Ektachrome 400 would be used but you should expect more graininess. Newer and better films are constantly coming onto the market, and it is best to ask your local camera store about the latest products.

Different film speeds.

PROCESSING

The money you spend on processing should depend on the circumstances. If you have taken a once-in-a-lifetime trip to Europe, you should get the best development service possible for your photographs. Kodak developing costs a little more, but is worth it. The author has found a wide variety of quality in cut-rate services. For slides of important events, the money saved with supermarket-quality service isn't worth the risk. If your photos were taken locally and you are on a tight budget, perhaps you may want to try cut-rate services. The author has used camera store quick development service for Ektachrome in order to meet a deadline. In most communities there are professionals or hobbyists who develop their own film. Sometimes they will develop your film along with their own for a small fee or sometimes free. It's worth exploring.

IMPROVING YOUR PICTURE TAKING

Technology has developed automatic 35mm cameras that set the shutter speed, f-stop (amount of light entering the lens), and focus. These have simplified photography to the point that the only major factor left to master is composition. To produce high-quality slides for a presentation, one needs to know something about basic photographic composition. The author is indebted to Eastman Kodak for many of the ideas presented here. If you can master the following compositional guidelines, your picture taking will be greatly improved.

Maintain simplicity. Have only one idea or center of interest in your picture. It must be clear to the audience what you want them to see. Several competing ideas in a picture will confuse the audience. Look for ways to give the center of interest in your picture the most visual attention.

Moving in close is one of the simplest ways to eliminate unwanted and distracting backgrounds. Backgrounds may be simplified by:

1. Taking a shot from a low angle and using the sky as a neutral background. This works well with portrait shots.

2. Seeking out simple backgrounds such as a concrete wall or the weathered boards of a building or fence.

3. Taking a high-angle shot (shoot down from a high spot), thus using grass, the sidewalk, the street, or soil as a background.

4. Throwing the background out of focus. This may be done by using what is called a narrow depth of field. Select a large lens opening (f 1.8, f 2) and a fast shutter speed (1/500 of a second, for example) and focus closely on your subject. The background will be fuzzy. Use this technique to eliminate all bushes, wires, and other unwanted background distractions.

Avoid vertical slides. Most projection screens are in the shape of a horizontal rectangle. Vertical slides will bleed off the top and bottom of the screen. Mixing horizontal and vertical slides necessitates moving the projector in so that the projected image of the vertical slides won't bleed off the screen. This greatly reduces the image size on the screen. Also, if you want to use slides on a video tape, they must be horizontal.

Use the Rule of Thirds. Divide your composition into six parts by imagining two vertical and two horizontal lines each dividing the image area into thirds (see illustration). Place your subject at the points where the vertical and horizontal lines intersect. Placing the subject off center results in a much more interesting composition. If you are photographing a moving object or person, show the subject moving into the composition. Do not place the subject dead center unless it is an extreme close-up or your subject has great visual impact. Don't place a horizon (such as the ocean) in the center, either.

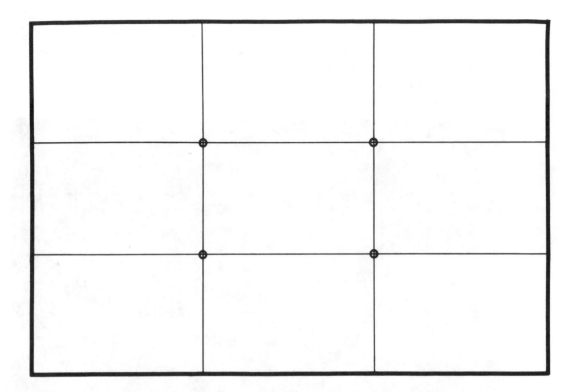

Rule of thirds.

Use lines. Seek to use lines—a road, fence, sidewalk, steps, shadows, or sun rays—to lead the viewer's eyes to the center of interest. Diagonal lines give a feeling of dynamics and action. A winding road forming an S (called S composition) will lead the eye to the subject of interest. Posing people so that their positions form a triangle or other geometric shape can also make your picture more dynamic.

The road leads your eye into the picture.

S-curve photo composition.

Use balance. Balance is a pleasing arrangement of shapes, colors, or areas of light and dark that complement one another. Balance is usually classified as being formal or informal. Formal balance involves placing an equal amount of material on each side of an imaginary line down the center of your composition. In informal balance a large object may be balanced by a small one through the use of space, as on a teeter totter when an adult is balanced by a child, with the child at the end of the board and the adult close to the fulcrum. An over-the-shoulder shot is an example of informal balance. A child clinging to the back of its mother is another. In the picture on this page two adults are balanced by a gladiolus.

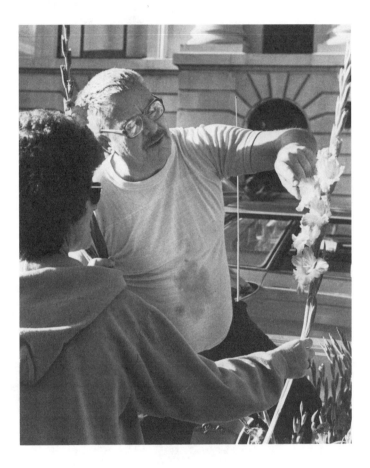

Informal balance.

Use framing. Objects such as a tree branch, an archway, or a doorway can be used to frame the center of interest.

Use of foliage as a frame.

The framing material is usually placed in the foreground in front of the subject.

Objects in the foreground frame the bulldozer.

When taking scenic slides, seek to place people or objects in the foreground to keep your scene from seeming flat and uninteresting. People in the foreground also give the viewer a reference as to the size of the scene you are photographing.

Avoid mergers. It is frustrating to have a roll of film developed only to find trees, telephone poles, or wires growing out of the heads of subjects. How does this happen? You see everything in three dimensions, but photographs are two dimensional. It is easy to focus upon the subject and forget about the background. Remember guideline number one—simplicity—and be aware of the background. Mergers also occur when you cut off the head or feet or cut people in half. Failure to align your eye properly with the camera's viewfinder may be the problem here, especially if you wear glasses. A merger may also occur if an object steals the attention from the center of interest. A bright red object in the background may draw the viewer's eye away from a subject. Look carefully at the background before you take a picture to eliminate all mergers.

Pole in background creates merger.

Consider continuity. When planning or shooting a slide/tape program, think in terms of a sequence of shots to tell your story. A long or establishment shot can orient the audience to where the action is taking place. A medium shot establishes more completely who is doing the action or clarifies the action that is taking place. Close-up shots portray the action in detail. Study TV and analyze the sequence of shots taken to tell the story.

Long shot.

Medium shot.

Close-up.

Extreme close-up.

Move in close. This is related to continuity. Beginners often do not use enough close-up shots. Moving in close solves many compositional problems and gives visual impact. If your program is demonstrating the steps involved in a skill, the audience must be able to easily see each step performed. Close-up shots enable them to do this. If you have a single-lens reflex camera, invest in a telephoto or zoom lens. This allows you to get good close-up shots without placing the camera under the subject's nose and avoids facial distortion in extreme close-ups. A good lens for

Moving in close solves many compositional problems.

portrait work is a 135mm. It is also easier to throw the background out of focus with a telephoto lens and thus avoid mergers.

Avoid stiff, posed shots. Have your subject doing something rather than looking into the camera lens. Talk to your subject and tell him or her the facial expression or mood you are seeking. Take shots of children and pets at their eye level, not yours.

Have your subjects doing something.

Vary the camera angle. Amateur photographers often take all shots at their own eye level. A variety of angles will add interest to your program. Try taking pictures from ground level, lying down on your back, or from a vantage point for a high-angle shot. An over-the-shoulder shot of someone reading a book gives a different feel from a frontal shot.

Bracket shoot. Sometimes when you are taking pictures for a slide/tape program you get into difficult lighting situations. Light reflecting off backgrounds, low-angle shots, or shots of a subject standing in front of a window can cause the camera to give a false light reading. Many times this results in the subject being underexposed. The problem can also occur when the subject is in a setting of mixed sunlight and shade. When you are not sure of the proper setting, take a shot using the light reading of the camera, then either open up or close down the lens a stop and take another exposure. By shooting with a number of aperture settings, you will probably get a correctly exposed slide. This may seem to be a waste of film, but if the picture does not turn out and you need it, how much does it cost to return to reshoot it?

Lighting

This book will not say much about flash photography because the emphasis is upon planning rather than photography. Kodak and other companies have published excellent books on flash photography which are available at your local camera store. However, you should be aware that one good use of flash is to provide fill-in light that can eliminate heavy shadows on a portrait in bright sunshine. Another way to eliminate heavy shadows is to use light reflectors. These may consist simply of a piece of white poster board, or aluminum foil crinkled up and taped to a piece of corrugated cardboard. This will reflect sunlight into the shadow areas and eliminate harsh facial shadows. Generally, someone must hold the reflector for you while you shoot the picture.

Without fill-in light the subject's face is heavily shadowed.

Fill-in light eliminates facial shadows.

Filters

Filters are very helpful in getting special effects for slide/tape programs. Filters are used basically to make photographic subjects look "right" and "better." One filter recommended for

Filters.

general use is a UV or haze filter, which reduces the bluish cast in scenic shots. It also keeps dirt out of your lens and protects it if it is dropped or hit. A polarizing filter can be used to darken a blue sky and intensify colors. It can also do away with reflections and glare caused by light reflected off glass, water, and nonmetalic objects. If you are using a single-lens reflex camera, the effect of the polarizing filter can be seen by looking through your lens. Turn the filter until you get what you want. You can see if the reflection has indeed been eliminated.

Filters can darken the sky and reduce haze.

Special effects may be obtained with filters. Diffusion filters will produce "soft" images and are great for portraits because they add mood, as well as reducing wrinkles in older people. Diffusion filters are available in various degrees of strength. Fog filters make normal scenes seem foggy. They are similar to diffusion filters and may be used to give photographs a pastel effect. Vignette filters give a sharp image in the center that becomes less and less sharp toward the edges. Star filters are called that because they turn bright reflections into four-, six-, or eight-point stars. You have seen these used in advertising, for example, to highlight the reflection of a chrome piece on an automobile. Multi-image filters are prism filters that produce multiple-image photographs. There are several types. One produces a center image surrounded by four or five segments of the same image. Contact your local camera store for more information. The use of filters can add interest and creativity to your slide/tape program.

CAMERA MAINTENANCE

Good photography requires maintenance and cleaning of lenses. Cleaning should always be done using professional photographic lens tissue or a soft camel hair brush. Your moist breath may be used with the tissue or brush, or use professional lens cleaner. Do not use paper towels or tissues that might scratch the lens. A haze filter on the front of your lens will simplify keeping your lens clean.

It is a good idea to have your camera batteries checked at least every six months. Camera stores will test them for you. A camera bag is a good investment to protect your camera and hold accessories. If your camera becomes inoperable, your local camera store will send it in to the proper repair facility. If you purchased your camera from them they often do this at their expense; otherwise you pay the shipping. Sometimes minor adjustments may be made at the camera store.

MODEL RELEASE FORM

If you are producing a slide/tape program which will be widely circulated, it is best to get a release signed by any subjects you photograph (see the model release form in appendix A). If you photograph disabled students, be sure to have signed parental approval before incorporating those slides into your program. "Valuable consideration" indicates that models are to be paid. If no payment is to be made, eliminate this statement from the release form.

4
Planning and Producing Graphic Slides

Graphic slides may be used in a presentation to explain difficult concepts which cannot be photographed. They may also be used to add visual impact and thus heighten the response of the audience. Graphic slides should be of the same professional quality as photographic slides. Later in this chapter we will present techniques and materials that will help amateur producers design professional-looking graphics.

FUNCTIONS OF GRAPHIC SLIDES

Graphic slides have a number of functions in a slide/tape program.

Reinforce the narration. Words appearing on the screen may reinforce key terms, definitions, quotations, and sayings. The audience members will remember what they see longer than what they hear.

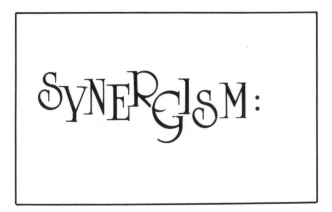

Words on the screen reinforce key terms.

Provide title shots. The title slide should describe the main idea being presented. Well-designed title shots add professionalism to a presentation.

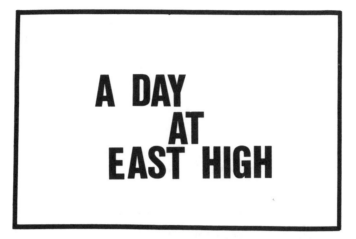

The title shot should describe the main idea of the program.

Provide credits. People like to see their names on the screen. A number of people may have helped you with your production—photographers, narrators, musicians, artists. If you have copied a photograph out of a publication, credit should be given to the photographer.

Thank people who have helped you.

Give important quotations. The audience cannot see quotation marks in a script. You can make sure they understand that you are quoting an important source by placing short quotes or key ideas, with attribution, on the screen.

```
          MURPHY'S LAW:

          If anything can go
          wrong it will
```

Let the audience know you are quoting a source.

Provide definitions. Technical terms, words not often used, words of Latin origin, medical terms, and the like may not be understood by the audience. Showing these words on the screen will help the audience recognize them and their spelling and visually reinforce the definition. This technique may also be used when you are going to use abbreviations widely.

```
          TECHNOLOGY:

          "The systematic application of
          scientific or other organized
          knowledge to practical tasks."
```

Reinforce the meaning of terms with a graphic.

Bridging gaps. Some things cannot be photographed or explained clearly with words—for example, the internal workings of a machine or instrument, the circulatory system, and the location of cities or countries. Graphics are often the best way to get such concepts across. Also, drawings can be used when a slide you had counted on did not turn out and you cannot retake it. Graphic slides can save you the cost of a trip and film to get just one shot.

Visualize operations. A flow chart, for example, can visualize the sequence in the manufacture of a product, or the way a bill becomes a law in a state legislature.

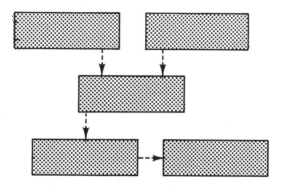

Charts can visualize a process.

Visualize foreign words. Because foreign words are often unfamiliar to audiences, visualizing them helps.

Fiche

nf. pin, slip of paper,
form, index-card, chit.

Visualize the spelling and meaning of foreign words.

Give contrasts and comparisons. Ideas may be contrasted or compared using a split screen with two images. Shapes, bulk form, and details can be visually compared using this type of graphic.

A split screen can visualize comparisons.

Introduce or review main ideas. Key or main ideas may be reinforced by progressively revealed graphics. If there are five main points in your presentation that you want the audience to remember, progressively present each word or phrase as you talk about it. How to produce progressively revealed informational slides will be explained on page 55.

WHY USE A TAPE RECORDER?

1. Makes teaching interesting
2. Cultivates listening habits
3. Self evaluation
4. Develops self-expression

Main ideas may be reinforced by a graphic.

Show labels. Often components of an object shown in a slide must be identified with labels, or motion must be indicated by arrows. There are various ways to do this. One is called a "double burn" (see p. 54).

Show maps. Too often we assume that audiences understand the location of cities, countries, or states. This may not be the case. The relative location and size of a geographic site may be visualized by using simple maps. Distances may also be made comprehensible by visually comparing them with local distances familiar to the audience.

Maps visualize location, size, and distance.

Show graphs. Pie charts, bar graphs, pictographs, line graphs, surface graphs, time lines, family trees, organizational charts, and area graphs may visualize relationships. Visuals conceptualize the importance of statistics, which are otherwise often dull and unlikely to be remembered.

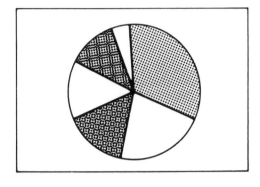

Pie Chart.

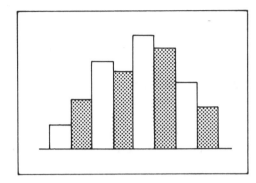

Bar Graph.

Pictograph.

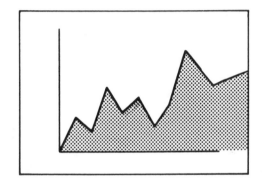

Surface Graph.

Move audience to desired actions or reactions. At the completion of your slide/tape program you may want to move your audience to a specific action. A graphic slide may present a possible action or project or ask a question pinpointing the audience's responsibility. Graphics can clarify for the audience what action you are seeking.

Use a graphic to motivate action.

LETTERING TECHNIQUES AND MATERIALS

The production of graphic slides will often involve lettering. In this section we will deal only with materials and techniques which are easy and readily available to students, teachers, and other individuals. Chapter 5 is devoted entirely to hand lettering.

Dry Transfer Lettering

Dry transfer lettering is the quickest, easiest way to produce professional-looking lettered graphics. It is available in white and black, in hundreds of styles and many sizes. When purchasing dry transfer lettering, try to match the style of lettering with the mood of your program. For example, if it is a Civil War topic, don't use a modern style. When placing letters on a sheet of cardboard, make faint guidelines. Space letters according to what pleases your eye; do not place letters the same distance apart. Study magazine ads for ideas on letter placement and spacing. Beginners often place letters and lines of type too far apart. This can hinder legibility. If there is an art store in your community, browse through it to discover different graphic arts supplies that may be helpful. Also try to get a lettering catalog. Chartpak is one company which markets dry transfer lettering. Use the catalog to select and order lettering. Notice that you can also get geometric forms such as circles, ovals, and squares; textures; various symbols; trees; human figures; and many other types of rub-on artwork. You can produce very professional graphic slides with these materials.

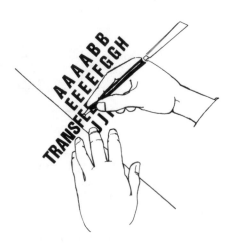

Dry transfer.

Dry transfer lettering is applied as follows.

1. Draw guidelines where you want the letters positioned. These lines should be faint and easily erased or they will photograph on your visual. You may use black letters on light cardboard or white letters on dark cardboard. Remember, sloppy work will be magnified when it is projected onto a large screen.

USE GUIDELINES

2. If you are using typing paper as a backing material for your graphic you may use a grid sheet under the paper on a light table. Grid sheets eliminate the need to erase guidelines. They also help you align materials vertically as well as horizontally.

3. Rub or burnish the entire letter to be transferred with a blunt object such as a used-up ballpoint pen or a burnishing rod (available at art stores). After you have rubbed the lettering onto the backing material, take the protective backing sheet and place it over the letters. Rub gently with your hand to affix the lettering.

4. If you make an error, letters may be picked up by placing a piece of masking tape over the error. Rub gently and then carefully pull up the tape. Care must be taken not to pull up part of the backing material with the letter.

5. After you have completed your artwork, tape a protective sheet of paper over it. This will protect it from dirt and damage until it is photographed and filed.

6. When you have finished, replace the lettering sheet in the plastic envelope in which it came or in a manila envelope. This will protect the remaining letters from damage and prevent them from becoming dry and brittle.

Stencil Lettering

Die-cut cardboard lettering guides are available at office supply and art stores. Trace the letters with a sharp #2 lead pencil. The centers of o's, e's, and a's are held in place with uncut cardboard strips that give the lettering the stencil look. Filling in this gap with a black or dark felt pen eliminates the stencil look. The letters may be colored with felt pens.

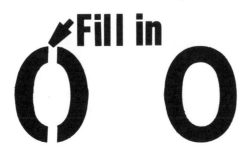

Die-Cut Lettering

There are many types of die-cut lettering.

Construction Paper Letters

These come in one-, two-, or three-inch-high sizes. They are available at school supply stores. Affix them to backing materials using spray adhesives or rubber cement. Don't use glue containing moisture, as it will buckle the letters.

Plastic or Mylar Letters

These are widely available in places such as office supply stores. They come on a cardboard backing and are adhesive backed. To use, peel off the backing material and affix to your artwork.

Gummed Letters

Sometimes called "Lick 'n' Stick," these are easily applied by dampening the glue on the back and rubbing them onto the artwork with a facial tissue. They are available in a number of sizes and colors and are often used to make signs, posters, and bulletin boards.

Heavy Cardboard Die-Cut Letters

These are available in, or can be ordered by, art stores. They may be purchased by the individual letter; thus you pay only for the letters you need. They may be laid over colored cardboard or magazine pictures for title slides. They may be used more than once.

Ceramic Letters

A number of types of ceramic lettering kits have been developed for home movie titling. Some have gummed backs. Ceramic letters are available in, or may be ordered by, photo stores. They are more expensive than other types of letters but may be reused many times. They give a three-dimensional look to slide graphics.

Typewriter

Newer typewriters usually have interchangeable fonts. Typed lettering may be used for labels and captions on photographs and drawings. Type on white or light colored paper. Cut out the

words using a steel-edged ruler and X-acto knife or razor blade. Affix to the artwork using spray-on adhesive. Word-processing computer equipment with a daisy wheel printer or high-quality dot matrix printer may also be used for labels, captions, quotes, and definitions. The state of the art in computers is constantly changing. Much more use will be made of this type of lettering in the future.

Sign-making Plastic Guides

These guides are sometimes called by the trade name of "Wrico." Kits containing plastic lettering guides and steel-tipped pens may be purchased at graphic arts stores. This is perhaps the easiest to use of the mechanical lettering devices, although it does take a little practice. The pen is held vertically to trace the letters in the plastic guide. The author has found that older students can master this type of lettering, sometimes better than teachers.

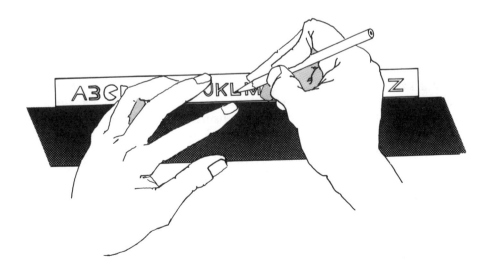

Wrico lettering.

Write-on Slides

Eastman Kodak markets the Ektagraphic write-on slides. These are 2 x 2-inch mounts containing Estar base plastic. The writing area is 1½ x 1½ inches. You can use marking devices to make title slides and other word graphics. Write-on slides are good for children to use when producing their own slide/tape programs. The major drawback is that they are not very professional looking.

ENHANCING GRAPHIC SLIDES

Many materials and techniques may be used to enhance and enliven graphic slides. While some of the materials listed below are used by professional graphic artists, anyone can use them to make professional-looking slide/tape graphics if the artwork is kept simple. Catalogs found at art stores or obtained by writing to the companies listed in appendix C offer a wealth of materials.

Poster Board

A simple way to make a graphic is to trace a drawing or lettering from a book or other printed source onto poster board. Coat the back of the tracing paper with #2 soft lead pencil carbon. Rub on carbon diagonally in at least two directions. Place the drawing over the poster board and trace. The image will transfer onto the poster board. Ink in with felt pens. You can add spots of color if you like.

Magazine pictures can be cut out and placed on poster board of a contrasting color. Affix to the poster board using rubber cement or spray adhesive. Captions may be added using lettering clipped from printed sources, hand lettering, traced letters, or die-cut letters.

A simple but pleasing graphic may be made by tracing a cartoon or simple line drawing onto typing paper. Ink in the outlines with a black felt pen. Add color to the drawing using colored felt pens. Cut out the drawing around the black outlines. Place the drawing in position on a darker colored piece of poster board and affix the drawing to the board with rubber cement or spray adhesive. A caption may be added using any of the lettering devices and techniques presented in this chapter. The white paper gives good contrast and has a vibrancy to it.

Chartpak Color Sheet

Chartpak markets a paper backing sheet made especially for artwork. It comes in a wide range of colors. Chartpak sheets will provide a much more vibrant background than poster board. Simple word graphics can be produced by using dry transfer lettering. White letters on a dark background or black on light background look professional. With a strong background color such as red, both white and black lettering may be used. In such cases the white lettering is dominant.

Colored Adhesive

This is available at art stores under a number of trade names. Sometimes known as color film, it is adhesive backed and is used to fill in large or small areas that do not need tonal variations. Use it according to the following procedure:

1. Cut a section of the film slightly larger than the area to be colored. It is best to use an X-acto knife. Slip the knife under the film and lift it off the backing sheet.

2. Position the film piece on your artwork. Generally, it is best to use illustration board.

3. Use a sharp X-acto knife to trim and peel off surplus film.

More than one layer of colored adhesive may be laid down to form unusual shades of color. Rub-on lettering may be placed over areas of color film. Certain types of felt pen also may be used to draw or write on the film. Here are a few ways to produce very simple but colorful slide/tape graphics using this material.

1. Highlight a word by using a rectangular piece of red film under the word. Use rub-on letters over the film.

2. Trace a simple line drawing (such as a drawing from a coloring book). Using the #2 soft pencil carbon method mentioned above, transfer the drawing to illustration board. Add colored adhesive to parts of the drawing (for example, dress, shirt, or hair).

3. Cut out a starburst from a large sheet of colored adhesive. Use rub-on letters to add a message or statistics you want to emphasize (for example, the amount of money needed for the project presented in the slide/tape program).

4. Professional-looking pie charts may be quickly produced by using pieces of colored adhesive.

5. Geometric forms of any kind may be highlighted by use of color film.

Adhesive-backed Textured Material

There are hundreds of different varieties of this material, similar to colored adhesive and marketed by the same companies. Some patterns and textures available are lines, crosshatching, screens (dot patterns), wood grain, bricks, burlap, denim, weave, and many others. Apply this material to artwork using the same technique as for colored adhesive.

Colored Tapes

These materials are much like Scotch tape, but they come in a wide range of colors. They are available in widths from 1/32 to 1 inch. They are adhesive backed and are applied by rolling out the length needed and cutting. Bar graphs, line graphs, time lines, and organizational charts may be produced using colored tapes.

Wallpaper Samples

Merchants often give away old wallpaper sample books. Samples make excellent background materials for creative slide/tape graphics. Use die-cut or transfer lettering to create title slides or word graphics on the samples.

Textured Found Materials

Simple but very creative graphics may be produced by using readily found materials as background. Die-cut or ceramic letters may be used on a wide variety of textures, such as dyed burlap, burlap sacking, sandpaper, scraps of patterned fabric, corrugated paper, vinyl shelf covering (contact-adhesive-backed paper), rug samples, scrap plywood, scrap paneling, screen, and rusty tin or iron. There are many other textures at your fingertips, such as chalk on a sidewalk;

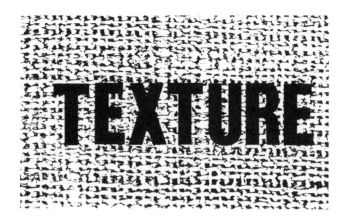

you must use your imagination. Use textures to make graphics that fit in with the theme of your presentation.

USING MAPS

Maps can help orient your audience when geography is relevant to the content of your program. Do not assume that audience members will know where Brazil is or where a U.S. national park is located. Simple maps will help to clarify such locations in their minds. Do not

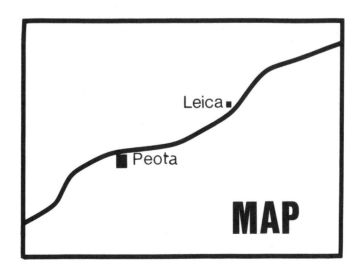

photograph oil company, encyclopedia, or state-sponsored maps. They have too much detail and can confuse rather than help. You may trace from such maps, eliminating unneeded details. Transfer onto poster or illustration board and then add color using colored adhesive or textures. If you don't have access to these materials use a yellow felt-tipped pen to highlight locations. Maps may also visualize the relative sizes of countries or states. Simply make outline maps of the two areas to be compared, and use, say, a red line to represent one country and a green line to represent the other. If one area is larger than the other, use yellow pen to color in the smaller to highlight it.

ENLARGING IMAGES

Sometimes you may discover lettering or a drawing that you would like to use in a slide/tape graphic but that is too small or detailed. If an opaque projector is available, it may be used as an art enlarger. Simply tack a piece of white paper to the wall and trace the enlarged image onto it. You can also make a photocopy, if the artwork is in a book, and use this as a master to make a heat copy overhead transparency. Then use the overhead projector as an art enlarger as described above. If heat copy overhead transparency equipment is not available, trace the image onto clear

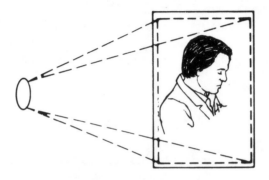

Enlarging an image.

acetate using a felt-tipped pen such as a Sharpie or Vis-a-vis; then project and trace the image. You may trace the image onto tracing paper and then coat the back with #2 soft lead pencil carbon and trace onto colored poster board. Ink in lines with black pen and then add color. Graphics on white typing paper, mentioned on page 48, may also be produced using this technique. Lettering found in magazines, books, and other printed material may be enlarged and used for quotes, headings, or captions.

REDUCING IMAGES

Today we are blessed with photocopying machines that are capable of reducing images. By copying a drawing several times, successively reducing it, a large drawing may be transformed into a very small one. If the original drawing was produced using thin outlines, however, it will not reduce well. Heavy outline drawings work best. These drawings can be given color and punch by using colored felt-tipped pens or using colored adhesive as mentioned above. You may want to mount the photocopy on heavy cardboard using rubber cement or spray adhesive. This makes it easier to work on and to file later.

HIGH-CONTRAST GRAPHICS

To prepare them for the slide/tape program, graphics must be put into slide form. One of the simplest but most professional-looking techniques for doing this is called high-contrast graphics.

Line drawings and lettering are copied onto a high-contrast film used by offset printers (see chapter 6 for how to use a copy stand). Kodak markets this film in a 35mm format called Kodalith Ortho. It may have to be special ordered by your local camera store. It is an extremely slow film with an ISO rating of six. It will not copy grays; any artwork will copy as either white or black negative. You will probably have to experiment with exposure times. When copied, lettering done in black pen or dry transfer lettering will show up as white lettering on a black background (a negative image). The white lettering may be projected as is or may be colored

using felt-tipped pens (which may give streaky color) or by leaving the negative immersed in food coloring for several hours or overnight, depending upon how dark you want the lettering. You can learn to develop this film yourself, or most camera stores can have it developed for you.

Offset printers with a large process camera can reduce images to 35mm size and photograph them onto Kodalith film. You will have to cut and mount the images yourself. The author has produced many high-contrast slides this way.

Double-Burn Slides

After you have a title photographed on high-contrast film (white letters on a black background), the film may be double exposed (the result is a "double burn") with a scenic slide to form a slide title. Ask at your local camera store for the name of individuals or companies who can produce double-burn slides.

A double burn places lettering on a slide.

IDEAS FOR USING HIGH-CONTRAST GRAPHICS

High-contrast slides can make your presentation more professional looking. Here are some ideas for using them.

1. Title slides.

2. Credit slides.

3. Progressively revealed slides. Let's say that you have four points you want to emphasize. Put the four points on white paper using hand lettering or black dry transfer lettering. Place the paper on a copy stand (see chapter 7). Cover with white paper all the points except the first. Make a copy. Uncover the second point and make a second exposure. Uncover the third point, and then the fourth point, making exposures each time. Thus on the screen your points will be progressively revealed.

To discuss following:

1. **Consider direct individual solicitation.**

To discuss following:

1. **Consider direct individual solicitation.**

2. **Consider cutting staff.**

To discuss following:

1. **Consider direct individual solicitation.**

2. **Consider cutting staff.**

3. **Consider having staff take pay cut.**

Progressively revealed slides.

4. Quotations. You can highlight a key word or words by coloring them.

5. Definitions. You can highlight the word to be defined by coloring it.

6. Words to songs. Use high-contrast slides to teach the words to songs, or project the words onto a large screen behind a singing group so that the audience enjoys reading the words as the group sings them.

7. Simple maps. Simple maps are sometimes easier to read if they are in high contrast (white lines on black background).

8. Logos and symbols. Sometimes logos will look better and more striking if they are reversed.

9. Masks. A photographic mask provides a method of cropping out unwanted portions of a slide by covering them. To produce a mask cut out a geometric shape such as a circle, oval, square, or diamond from black or red paper. To correctly position the geometric shape so the mask will be in the correct position on the slide, project the slide onto a sheet of 8½ x 11 white paper. Then affix the black shape in the correct position using double-edged tape. Photograph on high-contrast (Kodalith) film using a copy stand. The results will be a white geometric shape on a black background. Sandwich mount the mask and the slide.

Masks.

5
Hand Lettering

Slide/tape programs often must be produced on limited budgets. Graphic arts materials such as dry transfer lettering are expensive. If you have some artistic ability, hand lettering can be an economical way to produce title slides, credits, quotes, and other lettered graphics. Even if you don't have much artistic skill, you most likely can produce acceptable cartoon-type letters. The illustrations in this chapter have all been done by hand using a felt pen. Here are some pointers for drawing cartoon letters:

1. Begin by making guidelines to keep lettering straight and of uniform height.

2. Keep letters the same thickness throughout. Fat letters are preferable to thin.

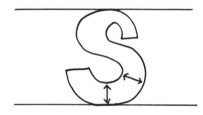

3. Don't try to make lettering outlines straight. Never use a ruler. Curved, flowing lines are more pleasing. It should be clear that the lettering is hand drawn.

4. Form the letters with downward strokes rather than by pushing upward. This gives you more control over the pen.

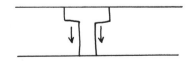

5. One-quarter-inch blue-line grid sheets are available at office supply stores. Use grid sheets and a #2 soft lead pencil to practice hand lettering techniques.

6. Imitate the hand-lettered alphabet at the end of this chapter. Trace it if you have to until you can draw it freehand. Practice doing the alphabet, then words.

7. After you have practiced with a pencil, try using a felt-tipped pen on scratch paper. Make different sizes of letters, following grid lines to keep them straight. Use a grid sheet under white paper on an overhead projector or light table. This will speed up your lettering.

Lettering Size

Most beginners produce graphics whose lettering is all the same size. Different lettering sizes can be used to emphasize or subordinate words or ideas. A technique often used by graphic artists is to place a phrase of smaller letters over or under one bold, large word. To emphasize a word, make it fat and large.

The Use of Line

Graphic artists often use line to emphasize a word. Here are some techniques using line:

1. Outline your lettering, following the shape of the letters. You may color in the letters or between the letters and the line. This creates reversal-type lettering having good contrast and vibrant color.

2. Use a wide-nib felt pen to make "wire" letters. Go around letters with a thin-pointed felt pen. Color inside the outline with yellow or light-colored pen. Move the pen in a circular motion when adding color for best results.

3. Give emphasis to two or more words by enclosing them in line. Color inside the enclosing line.

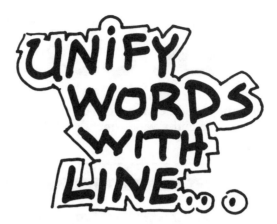

4. Words are sometimes enclosed by several lines. Color in between two lines to give emphasis to a word.

5. Use line to give a feeling of strength to lettering. Use pen lines to fill in outlined letters to give them strength. Texture effects may be done with pen.

6. Place lettering so that it breaks a horizontal line. The line will draw the eye to the lettering.

7. Placing a line above and below a word or phrase will emphasize it. Sometimes two lines are used, a thin one and a wider one.

Overlap Lettering

Larger letters can be used in a small space by overlapping the letters. This is a pleasing type of lettering and is easy to make.

Shadow Lettering

Another pleasing effect can be gotten by making shadow lettering. The lettering appears to have light shining on it from one side, thus casting shadows on the other side. This gives the lettering a three dimensional feel.

Capitals and Lower Case

Use all capital letters for headings and main ideas. Use upper- and lower-case letters to subordinate ideas and set them off from headings and main ideas.

Lettering Enclosed in Geometric Shapes

Placing lettering within ovals, squares, or rectangles will draw the eye and emphasize a word. The strongest geometric shape is the oval.

Be creative. Experiment with fitting lettering into various geometric shapes. Here are a few examples:

The Use of Color and Contrast

As with any other graphic arts techniques and materials, hand-lettered graphics should be colorful and have good contrast. Studies have shown that there are psychological associations with color.

Red arouses motor impulses and feelings (STOP signs are red).

Orange excites irritation.

Yellow/orange is warm, lively, and glowing.

Yellow arouses feelings of joy and gaiety.

Yellow/green is cheerful and spring-like.

Green is soothing and restful.

Blue is quieting, cooling; it expresses serenity.

Blue/green is sedate and somber.

Lavender is tranquil.

Blue/violet is stern, hard, and unyielding.

Purple suggests richness, royalty, and stateliness.

White gives the feeling of purity and immaculateness.

Black suggests gloom, darkness, and death.

Putting It All Together

Combining the use of lettering, line, shape, space, and color to produce a pleasing hand-lettered graphic will take some time and experience. Remember to keep it simple. Here are examples of hand-lettered graphics:

Four-grid-high lettering using one-quarter-inch grid sheet. This alphabet was drawn in about 45 seconds.

ABCDEFGHI
JKLMNOPQ
RSTUVWXY
Z1234567
8910

Three-grid-high lettering.

ABCDEFGHI
JKLMNOPQ
RSTUVWX
YZ 123456
7891O

Two-grid-high lettering.

6
The Use of a Copy Stand

If you own or have access to a copy stand similar to the one illustrated, you or your students can make slides from artwork or pictures found in magazines, textbooks, children's books, brochures, encyclopedias, and other printed materials.* Original student artwork or colored photo prints can also be copied. Copy stand photography is much easier than hand-held camera work; many of the usual photographic problems have already been solved. Whole slide/tape programs can be produced by students using only copy stand photography. There is a wealth of graphic materials on most subjects. Students will benefit by learning to choose what is and is not important to their message. A copy stand may be set up in one corner of the classroom and be used by students on an informal basis. Once the basic exposure has been calibrated, it is a simple matter to copy materials.

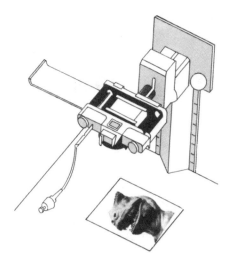

Copy stand.

---

*Note: Using copyrighted images without written permission may result in legal action. Consult a qualified legal advisor; this is a highly complex area of the law. Credit should be given to sources of artwork.

A copy stand serves three main functions: (1) it holds the camera steady while an exposure is being made; (2) it permits the photographer to adjust the camera's distance from the material so that artwork of varying sizes may fill the slide; and (3) it provides a method of holding the material to be copied. A copy stand is a valuable tool for gathering visual material for a slide/tape presentation. The kinds of materials that can be photographed are limited only by the size of the copy stand.

Many schools have district-wide production centers with copy stands and cameras for teacher use. Copy stands may be purchased at local audiovisual houses. Plans for a home-built plywood copy stand are available in a booklet on close-up photography by Kodak at your local camera store. A copy stand may also be made from an old photographic enlarger stand. Some tripods can be set up as copy stands. Material to be photographed may be taped to a wall and copied using the camera on a tripod. It is also possible to copy pictures out of doors using sunlight or light shade as a light source. Tape the artwork to a wall, lay it on a smooth, flat place, or have someone hold it. A macro lens (see p. 69) is handy for copying out of doors because of its flexibility. By using a fast shutter speed, just about anything can be copied using these techniques.

Two accessories should be used with the traditional copy stand—a cable release for the camera shutter, and a piece of nonglare glass. A cable release permits the use of extremely slow shutter speeds without jarring the camera and thus blurring the slide. Cable releases are available at local camera stores. The nonglare glass will hold artwork flat and also cut down the glare from the lights. Such glass is available at local glass shops. A polarizing filter is also a helpful accessory. It is used over the front of your copy lens and eliminates the glare from the lights (shiny spots on an illustration). These filters are available at local camera stores.

A single lens reflex camera is necessary for copy stand work; it allows you to see the exact image that will appear on the slide. A word of caution—some single lens cameras will copy slightly more than you see in the viewfinder. This may result in a slide that shows the white of the page or a portion of the copy stand board.

CAMERA ATTACHMENTS

There are four different attachments for single lens reflex cameras that are useful for copy purposes.

Supplementary Close-up Lenses

These come on sets with +1, +2, and +3 magnification. They attach much the same way as do filters, on the front of your regular 50mm camera lens. Close-up lenses may be used separately or in combination. A +1 and +3 would give a +4 magnification. The degree of magnification needed varies, of course, with the size of the artwork to be copied.

Extension Tubes

These are attached between the lens and the camera body. Usually they have either a screw-on or a bayonette-type attachment. They also come in three sections with +1, +2, or +3 magnification. They may be used separately or in combination.

Bellows

Bellows are more expensive than close-up lenses and extension tubes, but they offer continuously variable magnifications over a wide, extendable range. Both extension tubes and bellows use the existing camera lens and thus produce good-quality images. They also are capable of producing larger-than-life images.

Extension tubes and bellows.

Macro Lenses

Macro lenses may come in various focal lengths. They are designed to be in focus from approximately three inches to infinity. They are very handy for taking extreme close-up pictures of flowers, insects, leaves, and rocks out of doors. They speed up the copy process because you do not have to constantly add or take away close-up lenses or extension tubes but can focus in on varying sizes of artwork.

FILM AND EXPOSURE

A traditional copy stand is lighted with two or more floodlights positioned at a 45-degree angle to the copy board. If the floodlights are white, such as EBZ #2, then you must use

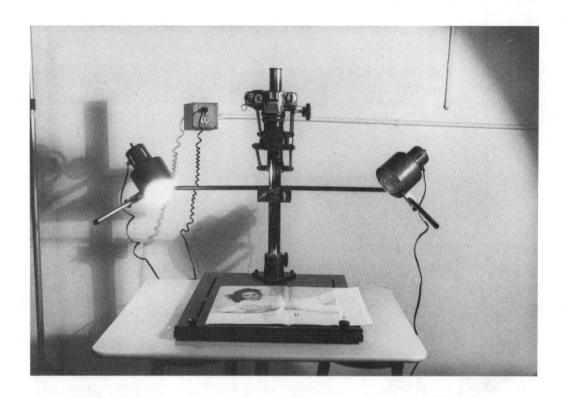

A copy stand set up.

Ektachrome 160 tungsten film, which is balanced for the warm incandescant lighting, in order to get the correct color rendition. Blue floodlights such as EWB #B2 will approximate out-of-doors daylight. Therefore, Ektachrome, Fujichrome, or Kodachrome outdoor film may be used.

If the copy stand is in a room lighted with fluorescent lights, turn them off before using the copy stand. These lights can affect the exposure. It is best to determine the exposure by using an 18 percent gray card, obtainable at a photo store. Lay it on the copy stand in place of the artwork—it will average out the lights and darks of the artwork. Setting the exposure directly from the artwork tends to result in underexposed slides. When setting up a new copy stand, take a test roll of film, making notations of shutter speeds and f-stops in a notebook. After the film has been developed, select the best exposure. Note on a card the calibrated exposure data and tape it to the copy stand. Most of your copy work will use this exposure setting.

POSITIONING ARTWORK AND LIGHTS

When producing or selecting artwork for 35mm slides, remember, the aspect ratio (proportion of height to width) is 2:3. Artwork not in a 2:3 ratio will not fit onto the slide and must be cropped or masked off (see appendix B). Artwork must be 6 x 9, 8 x 12, or 10 x 15 inches to have a 2:3 ratio. It is best to standardize copy stand artwork to, say, 6 x 9 inches. This is a good size to store in a steel file drawer, and the standardized size speeds up copying because you do not have to reposition and refocus the camera for each piece of artwork.

ASPECT RATIO:

2 : 3

The camera must be attached to the stand so that the film plane is parallel to the copy board. The artwork to be copied should be directly under the center of the lens. Strips of cardboard cut on a paper cutter may be taped to the copy board to form a frame. The frame's alignment on the copy board may be simplified by shining a pocket flashlight through the viewfinder of the single lens reflex camera. The light will project onto the copy board and reveal the area the camera will copy at this setting. Turn out the lights so that the room is dark. Move a white piece of paper around on the copy board until it is in the correct position. Then tape cardboard strips in the correct position. Then the artwork can simply be inserted against the cardboard stops and it will be in position for copying.

Lights should be placed at a 45-degree angle to the copy board. When setting up a copy stand for the first time you will have to experiment with the lamp-to-artwork distance. If the lamps are

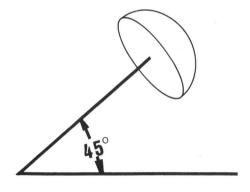

Copy stand light.

too far away sometimes paper surface textures will show up. If the lamps are too close objectionable reflections or glare may appear. Align the lights until there is an even area of lighting distributed over the copy board. When one of the copy lamps burns out, the new replacement lamp is usually brighter than the remaining one. To avoid uneven lighting, replace both lamps.

THE EKTAGRAPHIC VISUALMAKER KIT

The Ektagraphic Visualmaker kit was designed by Kodak for students and teachers who have little or no knowledge about copy stand photography. The kit includes a pocket camera,

Ektagraphic Visualmaker kit.

electronic flash, two copy stands with built-in close-up lenses, a pistol-grip handle, and a carrying case. The camera is attached to either stand with a screw knob. One copy stand is designed for copying 8½ x 8½-inch artwork. The second copy stand will copy 3 x 3-inch pictures. Operation is extremely simple. Place the camera and copy stand over the material to be copied and press the shutter release.

The large copy stand copies 8 x 8 inch artwork.

Lighting may be by three methods:

1. The electronic flash may be attached. It is calibrated for the correct exposure.

2. A flash cube may be used. A built-in reflector in the copy stand reflects just the right amount of light for correct exposure.

3. Natural light may be used. The later model kit cameras have electric eye exposure. Copy stands have holes so that the electric eye works on the stand. Thus copies may be made by using sunlight or light shade for lighting.

The Ektagraphic Visualmaker kit is a great tool for classroom use. Students can draw or clip artwork from magazines to illustrate topics they are researching and make presentations to students and parents. The author has seen slide/tape presentations produced by kindergarten children. For further information write to Eastman Kodak, Dept. 412L, Rochester, NY, 14650. Ask for the publication "Simple Copying Techniques with a Kodak Ektagraphic Visualmaker." The Ektagraphic Visualmaker is available at Kodak dealers and audiovisual dealers. Many schools have these kits available for check-out at the library/media center.

7
Audio Production

The quality of the sound track for your slide/tape program is important. Listening to a poor sound track is a frustrating experience. A good sound track will complement the message of the slides and set the mood that will move your audience to action. For very simple slide/tape programs, of course, sound tracks may be unnecessary. In fact, there is an advantage to live narration without taped musical background—the speaker can adapt the pace to the needs and makeup of the audience. But musical background, sound effects, and prerecorded narration do add professionalism to a presentation.

SUGGESTIONS FOR SELECTING MUSIC

Music at the beginning of your program or music that fades under the narration gives a polished feel to the program. Background music should support the message of your program unobtrusively. The music should match the style, tempo, and mood of your topic. Select music that complements and interprets the narration. If the narration is fast-paced or you seek a feeling of excitement use music with a lively tempo. You might even time a piece of music with a stop watch while you practice reading the narration.

Always keep the visuals in mind when selecting music. Certain pictures dictate the type of music needed. Be sure to devote adequate time to the selection of music.

A single musical piece used throughout your whole presentation can give an impression of unity. Guitar music is a soft, pleasing background for a slide/tape program. Vocal music, unless it reinforces words and ideas in the script, generally should be avoided, especially in narrated scripts. The use of several pieces can change the mood or pace of parts of your presentation. Sometimes it is effective to repeat the same piece of music several times throughout the program, especially if the passage is short. Repeating the lead-in music at the end will help give unity and reemphasize the mood of the program.

How do you go about selecting music for your slide/tape program? It is always best to acquire the help of experienced resource people. A disc jockey, radio announcer, music teacher or performer, music buff with a record collection, or library/media specialist may be of great help.

WHAT YOU SHOULD KNOW ABOUT COPYRIGHT LAWS

Although music can enhance your slide/tape program, the use of copyrighted music is risky. Use of "pop" music records or tapes without prior written permission from both the music copyright owner (generally the publisher) and the record company producing the record is illegal. You are required to request a synchronization license from the music copyright owner before use—this grants you permission to use the music with your slide/tape program. It is mandatory to obtain a written license in order to avoid infringement of U.S. copyright law.

Often synchronization rights are confused with performing rights. A radio or TV station pays to have a blanket ASCAP performing-rights license for the right to play recorded music on the air. Synchronization rights for slide/tape programs, video, and film are not included in such agreements. These must always be negotiated separately with the music publisher.

Negotiating with record companies for rights is a time-consuming process. If an artist is featured on a record, his or her permission must be obtained. Musicians must be notified and union pay regulations followed. Because of the hassle, slide/tape producers often seek to use original music or music in the public domain.

Most cases of copyright violations don't go to court. Generally they are clear cut, the accused is obviously guilty, and settlement is made out of court. You may object that you have seen many slide/tape programs using copyrighted music; this is undoubtedly true, but the use was still most likely illegal. It is best *never* to use copyrighted music for a presentation that will be shown to the public unless you have permission or have made contractual arrangements.

There are several solutions to the copyright problem:

1. Use music whose copyright has expired—that is in the public domain. Be aware, however, that *arrangements* can be copyrighted. A piece of music by a long-dead composer may still be a copyrighted arrangement.

2. Find a local musician to record original music or music whose copyright has expired.

3. Contract for the use of the copyrighted music. Generally, producers charge a fixed sum for the use of copyrighted music. The fee is usually set on the basis of a "per needle down" rate—a rate charged every time you place the needle down on a record to copy a section of music (or copy a selection from a tape). Thus, if you use lead-in music and fade-up music at the end of you program, you would be charged for two "needle downs." The cost varies from producer to producer.

4. Some companies specialize in sound effects and background music for films, video, and slide/tape programs. One such company is Thomas J. Valentino, Inc., 151 West 46th Street, New York, NY, 10036, telephone (212) 246-4675. The company offers a catalog of music classified by subject; this music may be purchased for unlimited use in slide/tape productions.

IDEAS FOR THE USE OF MUSIC IN A SLIDE/TAPE PROGRAM

While music is not essential to effective communication there are at least four advantages of using music in a slide presentation, some of which have been alluded to previously:

1. A musical lead into your presentation helps draw attention and establish your presentation.

2. Music can make your presentation more professional. Audiences have come to expect music in presentations through watching TV and films.

3. Carefully selected music can establish a mood or atmosphere that adds depth and richness to a presentation.

4. Music builds continuity and helps bridge transitions.

Music should be carefully selected so that it blends with the character and mood of your presentation. Here are a few ideas you might want to try:

1. Use various musical pieces to set the mood without any narration. Seek to change the slides to the beat of the music, and by using music with varying tempo, vary the pace of your presentation. This works well with scenic slides when you want the audience simply to enjoy their beauty. In this case words may hinder rather than help the desired effect.

2. Use music rather than continue a narration for a sequence of slides depicting something happening. The author used this technique effectively to present the erection of an office from the bare ground to the finished building, using a series of 26 slides set to fast-paced music.

3. Music may be faded up and a number of slides shown without narration to make a transition from one setting to another.

4. Music faded under a narration also sets the mood for a program.

5. Use music to reinforce the contrast of two ideas or periods of time. For example, in a program presenting the history of a community or state, use period music to emphasize the era a sequence of slides presents. The idea of past and present can be emphasized by using a piece of music from the past with a contemporary tune.

6. Care should be taken that the music is not too loud or too familiar; otherwise it might "fight" the narration rather than enhance it.

7. Instrumental music is preferable to voice backgrounds, especially solos. It is difficult to listen to a vocalist and narrator at the same time. However, if a piece of music presents the message you want to present, you may want to use vocal music and reinforce the message by placing the words on the screen as they are being sung. High-contrast slides work well for this. Slides may also be used with a singing group to reinforce the words to the songs they are singing. Don't use music from TV programs, commercials, or films with which the audience is familiar. For example, the *William Tell Overture* conjures up images of the Lone Ranger. The theme from *Chariots of Fire* has been used so often it has lost its effectiveness.

8. A good lead into or exit from a slide/tape program is a series of slides set to music. The tempo should be quite fast. A series of close-ups of faces or slides similar to the ones used throughout the presentation will interest your audience and give them a feel for what you will present. To exit a program, a fast series can be used to review some of the key ideas in your program.

PRODUCING THE SOUND TRACK

Because slide/tape programs have so many uses and levels of sophistication, sound track quality will vary greatly. For example, if students are producing a slide/tape program for a class report, the main function of the sound track is to communicate. A presentation produced by children for parents at back-to-school night may not be high quality, but will have a certain spontaneity and charm. However, a polished presentation that is to be taken out into the community as a fund raiser or to change public attitudes is another matter (see the next section, "Producing a More Professional Sound Track," as well as "Improving Sound Quality of Cassette Recorders," p. 93).

If students are producing a slide/tape program for in-class use, a sound track may be simply made using a cassette tape recorder and a record player or two tape recorders. The music is faded up or down by varying the volume on the record player or the second tape recorder.

Here are some tips for producing a sound track:

Recording Facilities

It is best to use a room with draped walls and carpeted floor. When this isn't possible use a room corner and hang blankets or cloth to form a recording booth. Place the mike on a stand or prop it up so that it is 6 to 8 inches from the narrator's mouth. Placing the mike on a blanket or

Place mike
6 to 8 inches away

pillow will absorb sound and help avoid sound bounce. In a classroom situation, a recording booth may be made from a refrigerator shipping carton. Glue egg cartons onto the inside and build a shelf for the recorder and mike.

Microphone Quality

Much of the quality of a slide/tape sound track depends upon the quality of the mike. For good quality, buy or borrow a good mike. Mikes sold with recorders most often will not give the best results.

Automatic Gain Control

Most recorders have this device, which modulates the volume while the machine is in recording mode. This feature helps the novice to get an acceptable recording even if the volume is not correctly set. However, automatic gain control will also work against you. If the mike is placed too far away from the narrator, automatic gain control will cause the mike to pick up unwanted noises, such as the motor of the tape recorder, movement of people, or cars going by. To avoid this, place the mike 6 to 8 inches from the speaker. The speaker should talk across the mike head, not directly into it. This will eliminate aspiration sounds.

Recording Tape

Use a high-quality recording tape. If the recording equipment you are using has Dolby or other capabilities, take advantage of them. Make sure that cassettes are held together with screws. These tapes can be taken apart and repaired, or if the tape comes off the reel it can be reattached. Because of the time and effort you put into planning and producing your program, it is self-defeating to buy low-quality audio tape. If you do not know what to buy, seek out stereo buffs or a library/media specialist for their opinion. If budget is a problem, sometimes radio stations and other businesses will donate used cassette tapes.

Sound Effects

Sound effects, especially at the beginning of your presentation, can be used to capture audience attention. Crowd noises, boat whistles, thunderstorms, a chugging locomotive, or animal sounds used wisely will hold the attention of the audience. Sound effect records may be available at your local library, record shops, school music departments, radio stations, and sometimes in the used record departments of Goodwill and Salvation Army thrift stores.

Practice

Time spent in careful planning will now pay off. Make one or two "dry runs" through your script before you record. Relax and speak in your normal voice. Beginners often read the script too fast, which results in a rushed feeling. Be careful not to rustle the sheets of the script or handle the microphone when recording.

The suggestions presented above may seem very simplistic, but the author has viewed some quality slide/tape programs produced on very simple equipment following these procedures.

HOW TO BECOME A SKILLFUL NARRATOR

The narration of your slide/tape program must not only be well written but should read well. If you do not have a pleasing voice, select someone else to do the narration. Record several friends reading a brief paragraph and then select the one whose voice is best suited to your needs. If you are to narrate the program yourself, use the following tips to increase your skill as a narrator.

1. Become involved with the true message of the script and to whom it is being conveyed.

2. Be believable. When you produce a narration, imagine that a member of your audience is sitting across the table from you.

3. Be involved with the words and phrases of the narration instead of just saying words. Your voice should evoke the mood and activities in the words. If the words are happy, smile as you read.

4. Do not be afraid to pause. Variety in pace makes listening more interesting and natural, and you will sound more conversational.

5. Make a practice tape and listen for pace, conversational tone, and naturalness of voice. Check to see if you have read the script too fast. Pencil notations on your script at points that need improvement. Underline words to be emphasized.

6. Narrate in a natural voice, the way people talk. Avoid a monotone. Emphasize words with your voice. Even at this point, you can revise your script if you find rough spots or phrases that can be deleted because they do not add meaning to the script.

7. Use body movement as you narrate. Gesticulate as you would if you were relating your message to family and friends.

8. Hold your script at eye level and talk just past the mike, not directly into it. Assume a comfortable posture, whether seated or standing.

Remember, if your voice does not sound pleasing or lacks the quality needed to establish the mood desired in your program, don't hesitate to get someone else. Record a number of voices onto tape. Keep them on file and play them when you are seeking someone to narrate a program. Be sure to identify each voice.

PRODUCING A MORE PROFESSIONAL SOUND TRACK

There are times when a highly professional sound track is needed. In some situations a great deal of mixing of sound is necessary: on-location interviews with people must be mixed and inserted into a narration, or sound from a number of sources must be mixed with music into a sound track. If you are going to mix sound from a number of sources such as interviews, it is best to use a reel-to-reel recorder to make the initial tape. Mixing requires the production of several generations of tape before the final product is obtained. Cassette recorders, unless they are of exceptional fidelity with a high-quality mike, will not give a final tape of acceptable quality.

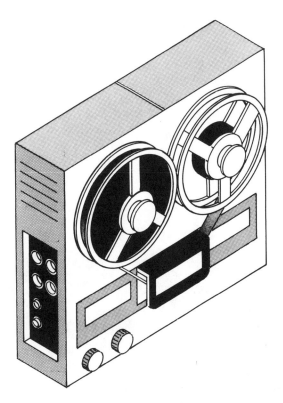

Reel-to-reel recorder.

Obviously, mixing requires professional equipment. There are several ways to get access to such equipment. One is to find an audio buff who has high-quality home stereo equipment and the skills to produce quality tapes. Another possibility is to utilize a local radio station.

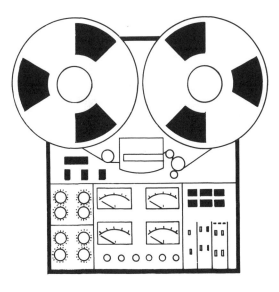

Stereo recorder.

Announcers are skilled in narrating scripts, and radio stations also have the equipment to mix sound. The author has often used the services of radio stations to produce slide/tape sound tracks. If your project is part of a community service program, people or organizations may donate their services. Otherwise, it is best to negotiate with several people or radio stations on the cost of production. Be sure that you have a contract that clearly spells out exactly what you expect so that misunderstandings don't occur later.

If you want to learn how to mix sound yourself and to become involved in producing more complicated slide/tape programs, you may rent or borrow a mixer. Audiovisual houses and

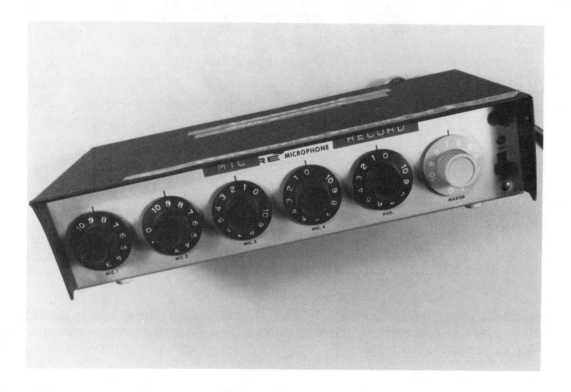

Audio mixer.

stereo shops sell mixers, should you want to buy one. The author has found that organizations sometimes seek someone to produce a slide/tape program; if you have the equipment and a little experience you can pay for the equipment by charging for your services.

8
Assembling Your
Slide/Tape Program

SORTING YOUR SLIDES

Once you have taken all the shots designated by your story board cards or production script, you can begin selecting the slides you will use. There are several ways to illuminate slides while selecting them.

1. Slide sorters are available at photo and discount stores. They must be set up by the purchaser and include a frosted (whitish) piece of plastic with ledges on which to place the slides. A light bulb is placed behind the plastic to illuminate the slides.

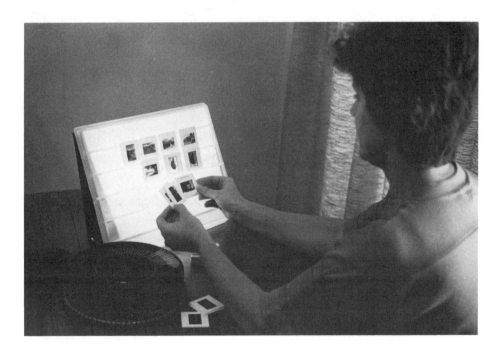

2. An overhead projector may be used as a slide sorter by placing white paper on the projector to cut the glare. Lay the slides out for sorting.

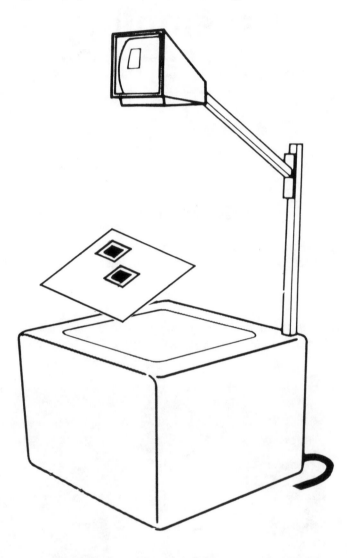

Overhead projector as slide sorter.

3. Light tables are used by graphic artists and are available at graphic arts stores or offset printing equipment companies. You can also make your own. It could be as simple as a cardboard box with a fluorescent or regular light bulb inside, covered with a piece of plate glass. Cement blocks or brick can also be used to raise the glass to the proper height. Used plate glass is sometimes available at glass stores. Glass companies will sandblast glass to frost it so that the light is diffused, or thin white paper can be glued to the underside of the glass.

4. Plastic slide sheets, including punched holes for three-ringed notebooks, have pockets to hold 20 slides. After the initial selection of slides, a good technique for setting up a slide/tape program is to number the pockets for as many slides as there are in your program. By laying this on a light table, you can visualize the progression of slides. You can try inserting alternative slides to see if a better sequence is obtained. These plastic sheets are available at photo stores. Easy storage is the big advantage of these sheets.

The first thing to do when sorting slides is to *throw away all poorly exposed slides.* Even one poor slide will greatly detract from the effectiveness of your presentation. Retake the photograph, or use a graphic slide to replace one you can't retake. The exception to this rule might be student slide/tape programs that will have limited use—however, students should learn to do quality work.

Once you have culled your slides, lay them out in the order specified by the storyboard. Rearrange the slides until you have the best continuity possible. At this point you may want to revise your script to tie in better with your slides. Seek to have sequences of slides rather than a jumble of unrelated slides. In a sequence of slides, avoid continual changes in background, lighting, and horizons. In chapter 3 we mentioned bracket shooting and taking several shots for each one designated on your storyboard cards. This pays off now, because you can choose the slide having the best exposure and composition. If you have only one slide per planned storyboard shot and it isn't any good, you face a time-consuming reshoot session or the possibility of writing the slide out of your script.

SEQUENCING YOUR SLIDES

Next, look at the objectives you wrote before you started production. Analyze your program. Does it meet the objectives? Ask yourself these questions about each slide: Does the image help me achieve my communcation objective? Is the slide clear and sharply focused? Does it blend with the narration and visualize the desired idea? Is the composition pleasing, having a center of interest and visual impact? Is there good continuity between slides, a good sequence that tells the story well?

INSERTING SLIDES INTO TRAYS

After you have put your slides into the best sequence possible, place them in a slide tray. If you are using a Kodak Carousel projector, here is the correct procedure for inserting the slides:

1. Face any wall and hold the Carousel tray in front of you grasping the number one slot at your right hand at first. As you insert slides, rotate the tray so the slot to be filled is always in your right hand. You will place the slides into the Carousel in order following the numbers on the slots.

2. To insert the slides, look at each in turn. If the image is in correct position (not backward), turn the slide upside down and insert it into the tray. (You can determine whether the image position is correct by three methods: Processor labels [such as Kodak] are placed toward the wall. Slides with lettering should be readable as the slide faces you. Sometimes neither of these tests is possible. If not, hold the slide up to the light and try to determine the emulsion [dull] side. Place the emulsion side toward the wall.)

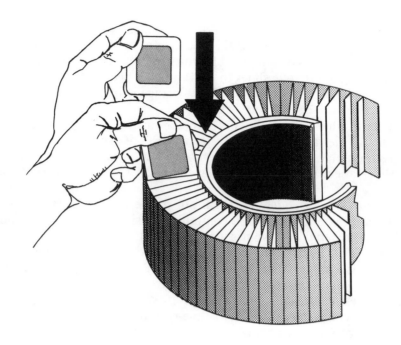

3. Put a dot in the upper right hand corner of each slide so you will always be able to tell at once if any slide is in the correct position.

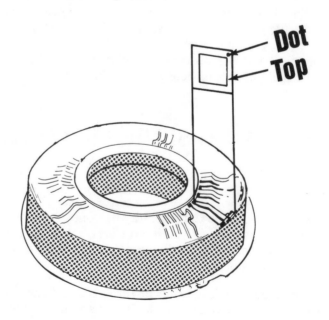

4. Number each slide with a soft lead pencil in the upper right-hand corner after the slides are in the tray. (Remember they are upside down.) If you spill the slides out of the tray and they are not numbered, it is a tedious task to replace them. Keep the lock-in ring in place on the tray at all times unless you are placing slides in the tray.

SEEKING FRIENDLY CRITICISM

Now, project your slides onto a large screen. Read the script to see how the slides and narration fit together. It is best not to make your final taped sound track until all the slides have been placed into the planned order. You still may have to revise the script several times. It is a good idea to leave your program for a day or so and come back with a fresh viewpoint to make revisions. A sympathetic friend can also be of help in evaluating and making revisions at this time.

Once you have taped the narration, have a friend or friends give you feedback on several things. How is the pace of the presentation? Is it too fast? Does it drag? Does the pace vary or does it plod monotonously? Are the graphic slides on the screen long enough to be read by the audience? Are any slides on the screen too long? Is the sound track clear and level? If there is music under the narration, is it unobtrusive or does it distract from the narration? (You may want to use the presentation evaluation form in appendix A.) Don't be defensive if your friends make suggestions for improving your program. Listen carefully. You don't have to follow all their suggestions, but remember that they have a fresh perspective. This is the time to revise again. It is better to spend time revising now than to be embarrassed later. This is especially true if your presentation is to be made to the general public or deals with important issues. Slide/tape programs produced by students in the classroom for one-time use naturally would require less critical evaluation.

SINGLE-PROJECTOR SYSTEMS

The result of your hours of planning and creative activity will be a potentially effective audiovisual program. Now the success or failure of your presentation depends upon the attention and planning given to the projection of the program. Most classroom use of slide/tape presentations will be restricted to a single-projector system, consisting of a projector, cassette recorder, and screen. The Kodak Carousel is probably the most commonly used projector in school systems.

Kodak Carousel projector.

We will discuss multi-image systems on page 90. Here are some tips for setting up a single-projector system.

1. To determine the proper screen size for the audience size, measure the distance from the screen to the person in the last row of the audience. Divide this by 6 to determine minimum screen size. For example, say the distance is 30 feet. Thirty divided by 6 equals 5 feet. Thus the minimum screen width is 5 feet.

$$30 \div 6 = 5$$

2. Lenses of various focal lengths are available for Carousel projectors to give the proper projector-to-screen distance. A good accessory to have is a zoom lens, which will give flexibility in filling the screen with the image from various distances.

3. The screen should be placed high enough so that the image will not be blocked by the audience. The projection beam should hit the screen squarely. If the projector is placed to one side and does not project squarely, a fan-shaped image called keystoning will result. The projector must usually be propped up. Generally a small table set on top of a larger one will do the trick.

4. Slides can be projected onto a translucent screen from behind the screen. A rear projection screen can be made by sandwiching a sheet of tracing paper between two panes of glass. Commercial rear projection screens are available at audiovisual supply stores. A rear projection screen is helpful in situations in which a small group is viewing the presentation and room darkening is not desirable. It is also handy for instructional purposes, when the projector may be stopped for discussion or for students to complete an activity on a work sheet.

There are a number of ways to combine narration and slide advance when presenting your program. Here are some basic ideas.

Use a marked script. You may advance the slides as you read from the script. The script should be marked at points where you are to advance a slide. The slides are advanced by the remote control mechanism found with most Carousel projectors.

Deliver an illustrated lecture. You may want to memorize your presentation and give it live as a lecture. You can then vary the pace with different audiences or stop and answer questions, review, or expand on a point. Advance the slides using the remote control mechanism.

Use audio cues for manual advance. Audible tones may be placed on the tape at the time it is produced. This may be done by using a toy xylophone, clicker, or electronic tone generator. Tone generators are available at audiovisual supply houses and are commonly used for manual advance with filmstrips.

Use inaudible signals for automatic advance. Cassette tape recorders with built-in synchronizers are sold at audiovisual supply houses or photo stores. Many times library/media centers have such recorders available for check-out. Signal generators are used to superimpose 50-or 1000-Hz signals onto the cassette tape. A special button on the machine records the signal on the tape when you press it. For playback, the tape recorder is connected to the projector by a cord. The taped sound track automatically advances the slide projector at each signal.

Cassette programmer.

MULTI-PROJECTOR SYSTEMS

The most common multi-projector system involves the use of a dissolve unit with two or more projectors. Dissolve control can greatly expand the visual impact of a slide/tape program.

Dissolve unit.

A manual dissolve unit is inexpensive and simple to use. Generally a sliding control bar is used to fade out the image projected by projector A and fade in the image on projector B. Some manual controls allow you to do cuts (instant transitions from one slide to another) and to vary the speed of the dissolve. By sliding the bar to the center, you can project both A and B images. Thus, for example, a high-contrast slide with lettering can be superimposed over a scenic slide.

Programmable dissolve units may be used with cassette tape recorders. As mentioned before, these machines place an inaudible pulse onto the tape, which when played back activates a slide advance or dissolve unit. Units vary in their ability to vary the speed of the dissolve. The chief advantage of programmable dissolve units is that your program will play automatically and can be used by someone else without audible beeps or a script.

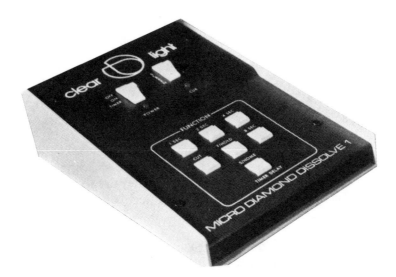

Dissolve unit.

When using two projectors, it is best to stack them piggyback on a projector stand. Projector stands are available at audiovisual supply houses or can be homemade. Both projectors must have lenses with the same focal length or two zoom lenses. The light beams from both projectors are aligned so that the images from projectors A and B are precisely superimposed. Focus slides designed especially for aligning the images are available commercially through photo stores or may be made by copying a graphic having grid lines so that projectors A and B have identical slides for set-up focusing.

If you can round up enough equipment, a more visually dynamic presentation may be made using multiple screens and projectors. Multi-screen presentations are effective in changing attitudes and motivating audiences. Images may be shown from different angles simultaneously, a single view may be produced on three slides to give a panoramic shot, and graphic and scenic slides may be juxtaposed. Perhaps you have seen some of the multi-screen programs produced by the Eastman Kodak company. For further information on multi-image production, the book by Eastman Kodak, *Images, Images, Images* is recommended. It is available at local camera stores or by writing for Kodak publication number S-12, Motion Picture and Audiovisual Markets Division, Rochester, NY 14650.

PREVENTING EMBARRASSING MOMENTS

Once you are satisfied that your slide/tape program is ready to take to the public, there are several practical issues to consider. Let us say that you have been invited to show your presentation to an organization. You must bring not only your slide/tape program but all the equipment to show it. The author has learned many painful lessons by forgetting some small detail. Here are some tips for preparing to take your presentation to the public.

1. Do *not* use your master tape for the presentation—store it in a safe place so that if a tape is damaged another copy can be made. Bring at least two copies of your sound track to the presentation. If one copy is damaged, you have a spare. The author has had a tape snag just before the presentation was to begin. Without a spare you are out of luck.

2. Punch out the two tabs on the backs of the cassettes you are using for presentations. This makes it impossible to accidentally record over the sound track. If you wish to revise the sound track, cover the tab holes with heavy masking tape.

3. Take along two heavy-duty extension cords and several three-pronged adapters. You cannot assume that the facilities where you are showing your presentation will have electrical outlets in handy locations or that they are the three-prong type. An electrical outlet bar or box having four or more outlets is necessary for plugging in projectors, recorders, and dissolve units.

4. Have spare projection lamps for each projector. Without a spare, it is disastrous to have a projection lamp burn out just before or during a presentation.

5. Always bring a small pen flashlight that fits into your coat pocket or purse. Use it for checking equipment in emergencies or to follow the script. It may save you from having to stop the program and ask for the lights to be turned on.

6. Practice making your presentation until you can run it manually if necessary. You will immediately know if something isn't right and can correct it. Have a copy of the script handy.

7. Carry a roll of duct tape. Tape down any cords that are placed where someone might trip over them. Try to run cords away from traffic areas. Duct tape is also useful for making emergency repairs.

8. Arrive early at the location where you are to make the presentation. Give yourself time to be prepared and relaxed. Try to have someone at the location assist you. A person familiar with the facility can be of great help in setting up the screen and projector. You also may want to patch into the PA system. Often someone like the custodian will know where and how to do this.

9. If your slide/tape presentation is only a part of the program you may have to move the screen to one side after you have set up your equipment. Use duct tape to make an X on the floor or carpeting where the center of the screen is to be located. Taped guide marks will speed the final set-up.

10. If you have arrived well before the audience is expected, make a trial run of at least part of your program to see that everything is functioning properly. Move around the room to test the sound level. If you are patching through a PA system, someone else with experience may know the proper setting.

11. Locate all of the light switches, or delegate someone familar with the location to turn out the lights. In some cases you may need more than one person. Having some of the lights on at the start of your program can distract the audience and ruin the desired effect of your program.

IMPROVING THE SOUND QUALITY OF CASSETTE RECORDERS

If you are using your slide/tape program in the classroom, then most of the foregoing ideas won't be needed. However, you may face a different set of problems. Teachers often have only small cassette tape recorders for classroom use. Such recorders have three- or five-inch speakers, and when the volume is loud enough for the class to hear, the sound is distorted. There are some ways to improve the sound of cassette recorders. First, as stated earlier, use a good mike when making the sound track. Second, use a larger speaker. Here are three suggestions.

1. Connect a 6 x 9 inch extension speaker to the output (speaker) jack of your recorder. On many small recorders, the speaker projects the sound vertically to the ceiling and then bounces it back to the audience. A free-standing extension speaker like those used with stereos will project the sound straight out to the audience.

2. Use a patch cord to connect your recorder to a transcription player or 16mm projector with a built-in PA system. You will find a jack input marked "mike" or "PA." Patch cords may be purchased at radio and TV stores. There are a number of different jack systems, and you may have to take your equipment to a stereo shop so that they can provide the proper patch cord. Plugging into equipment with PA capability reamplifies the sound so that your small recorder can be used for presentations to large groups.

3. Have a radio/TV technician make a power speaker by wiring a large speaker with an auxiliary amplifier. Amplifiers from discarded AV equipment will often work. Have the technician solder a cord to the speaker terminals and fit a jack plug to your recorder. This means that you can plug your small recorder into a very large speaker. The amplifier will reamplify the sound. Using a large power speaker, a small cassette recorder may be used in a large auditorium.

FILING YOUR SLIDES

Perhaps the reason slides are not used extensively in the classroom is that they require some type of storage and retrieval system so that the right slide can be located when needed. Without a filing system slides can become very unwieldy. The plastic 20-slide pocketed holders that can be stored in a three-ring notebook are useful for storage. Carousel trays can also be used. Each tray has a chart on which can be written a description of each slide in the tray by number. In this way you may store hundreds of slides on a single bookshelf. You may want to store slide/tape programs produced by the class in the library/media center for other classes to use.

If cost is a factor, slide files may be made from empty aluminum foil or waxed paper boxes. Fasten the cassette tape, enclosed in a plastic case to keep dust out, to the box with a rubber band. Several of these boxes may be placed in a large soap box and labeled according to subject or other classification system. Many boxes or trays of slides may be stored in an apple box which has been covered with patterned shelf vinyl (such as Contact). Thus in a small space, thousands of slides may be stored.

9

100 Ideas for Using Slides and Slide/Tape Programs in the Elementary School

KINDERGARTEN OR FIRST GRADE

1. Take pictures of all the school personnel—teachers, cooks, principal, janitors—so that children entering will know who these people are.

2. Use a slide/tape program to show the students on visiting day what will happen on the first day of school. This can help dispel the mystery and fear of the first day.

3. Produce a slide/tape about yourself, the teacher, to introduce yourself to your new class. Have pictures of your family and pets.

4. On the first day of school have a slide/tape program to acquaint students with the type of activities they will be doing throughout the school year. Keep a camera handy to take shots of the class this year to show next year.

5. Shoot a set of slides of the class on the first day of school. Use a quick development service. Project the slides to help the teacher and students learn everyone's name quickly.

6. Take pictures of students and activities throughout the school year. On the last day of school invite parents to view the highlights of the year.

7. Take shots of your classroom activities to be used for back-to-school night. Use to explain objectives and projects to parents.

8. Have slides of classroom activities to show to parents while they are waiting to meet with you individually. Some projectors can be put on automatic projection or use a remote control to let the parents change the slides at their own pace.

9. When assigning special projects such as in art, social studies, or science, have slides of projects that students have done before to give current students ideas.

10. Take dramatized pictures of a fire drill, tornado alert, etc., to teach children what they should do in case of an emergency.

11. Use a slide/tape program to introduce a unit of study. Copy materials from books, magazines, newspapers, and other sources to introduce the unit.

12. Take pictures of key things you want students to see during a field trip. Use to introduce the field trip and make viewing assignments. Use slides also to review and discuss what students have seen.

13. Take pictures on a field trip. After they are developed ask students to put them into the correct sequence and tell about the field trip as they show the slides. The field trip can be divided into different aspects for several groups to work on.

14. Have students draw pictures to tell about their activity in class. Use a copy stand to copy the pictures onto slides. Have each student narrate his or her picture. Use to show to parents for back-to-school night.

15. Play a musical record. Have students illustrate their feelings about the music. Copy their drawings onto slides and present to the class. Use as a rainy day activity when students can't go outside.

16. Play a story record. Have students role-play the story. Take shots of students acting out the story. Place the slides in a tray and use the record as the sound track.

GENERAL ELEMENTARY CLASSES

17. Use the shots you have taken of, say, your fourth-grade class. On the last day of school use as an orientation for the third-grade students assigned to you next year to give them an idea of what they will be doing in your classroom.

18. When you go to workshops or conventions, take slides or prints of displays, projects, and ideas presented. Use to remind you to use these ideas in your classroom.

19. If your school district does not have money for field trips, shoot slides of what students would have seen and use as a slide/tape program. Such programs are usually not available commercially and are of local interest.

20. On rainy days when children can't go outside, show slides of international trips you have taken. Use background music from the country or countries as you narrate the slides.

21. When you are taking shots of classroom activities, take them at the child's-eye level. This may mean getting on your knees. This will give a different perspective to slide/tape presentations you make to parents and to chidren.

22. State historical societies or museums often have historical photographs of your state or city. You may be able to copy them for use in teaching local or state history. The Ektagraphic Visualmaker kit (see chapter 6) is a handy tool to use to copy these pictures.

23. Lay out on a light table slides taken during the school year. During the last week of school ask students to select and arrange a slide program called "Thanks for the Memories." Use this song as background music as they show the slides.

24. There are a number of rare children's books that are no longer in print or available. Copy the illustrations onto slides and read the story onto tape for special treat occasions.

25. To teach the four seasons, take shots from your classroom window of the trees, lawn, or flowers outside during the year. Project without comment or with background music to visualize the four seasons.

26. Work with your library/media specialist to produce a slide/tape orientation to the library. Orient students to services and the location of books and materials.

27. If you assign special research projects in the library, produce a slide/tape program presenting step by step the procedures to follow in completing the project.

28. For special holidays, read a holiday story to the class. Assign each student to make one or more drawings illustrating a part of the story. Copy the artwork onto slides. Record each student telling his or her part of the story. Use these programs in the future for holiday materials.

29. Photocopy a story from a book onto slides. Only copy the first part leading up to the climax. Ask students what they think will happen or how the story ends. This can be used for oral communication development or as a springboard into an art project.

30. For current events, copy photos out of magazines of famous people in the news. Project and use to discuss who these people are and what they are doing. Use to acquaint students with national and state leaders.

31. Often there are special community events held during summer vacation. Some may be of a historic or ethnic nature. Use slides of the events to explain the cultural, ethnic, and historic background of the community.

32. Read the local newspaper carefully for stories about special people in the community who have made trips or have special skills or backgrounds. Invite them to speak to the class and show any slides they have, or go into the community and photograph them in action. Have them show the slides as they speak to the class.

33. Assign a group of three to four students to take a nature walk in the community or on the school grounds. Have them take an instamatic camera and a tape recorder, and have them record brief comments about the things they photograph. Get the slides developed and use the tape recording as the sound track. Have students give this presentation to the class.

34. Use slides to visualize playground rules. Pose students to illustrate the meaning of the rules.

35. To teach map reading, make a map of the school and local area. Display it on the classroom wall. Take slides or colored prints of buildings and sites represented on the map. Project the slides or mount prints to the map to illustrate what symbols on the map represent and what they look like.

36. To teach personal grooming such as combing hair or brushing teeth, take slides of students doing these activities (at their eye level). Have them write a script and make a presentation to the class.

37. To stimulate reading, post a list of 15 to 25 books to read. Give students several months to read these books. On the copy stand photograph one page from each book. The page should present an important character or event. Project the slides and ask students to identify (on a worksheet) the title of the book. The student identifying the most books receives a very special prize.

38. Photograph students or objects in groups of one to ten. Project and use to conceptualize the numbers from one to ten. Simple math facts such as addition or subtraction can be reviewed by photographing a grouping of objects.

39. Teach figurative speech such as "as bright as," "as cold as," or "as hot as." Take slides that illustrate these ideas. Project the slides randomly and ask students to match the figurative expression with the correct slide.

40. For creative writing, take a series of slides (you can use the copy stand and magazine pictures) of people, places, things, and actions. Select and project four slides and ask students to write a brief paragraph about each slide. You will have enough slides to use this activity with variations for a number of writing sessions.

41. Copy pictures of cities and locations around the United States onto slides. Mount a large map of the United States onto the wall. As you project slides of locations, ask students to go to the map and point to the locations on the map.

42. Give a student or students a pocket camera. Ask them to cover a news event just as a local newspaper reporter would. Ask them to take shots and write an article. You may want to use print film and mount the pictures on the article.

43. To teach appreciation of poetry, give students a copy of a poem having a lot of imagery. Give them a camera and ask them to illustrate the poem. Project the slides and read the poem as the narration. The narration may be taped with background music as well as words.

44. To teach geometric form, draw a number of geometric forms on a sheet. Give a copy to students. Assign groups to take a pocket camera into the community and photograph objects illustrating each geometric form on the sheet. They will then project the slides and give a report to the class.

45. Use the slides just mentioned with another class at a later date, having students identify each geometric form presented in the slides.

46. Have students give visual book reports by using the Ektagraphic Visualmaker (see chapter 6) to copy slides of the book jacket, cover, and illustrations. Students then make a visual report to the class. They may be assigned to write a script rather than a report.

47. Ask students to plan a pretend vacation. They then must research pictures of the locations in their vacation. Copy these onto slides and also have students take photos of the student "taking the vacation." Intersperse pictures of the student with the scenic shots. The student plans and writes a script. The student can pretend to have actually been to these places.

48. Have students write a poem, limerick, or haiku. Give students a camera and ask them to take shots illustrating the feeling or ideas in their poems. The poem is read onto tape and may include mood music. Use these presentations to stimulate other students to write poetry.

49. A backhanded way to teach spelling is to have students make signs featuring misspelled words on white paper with felt pens. Signs are copied onto slides and used in a fun drill in spelling.

50. A good source of slide material is postcards. Whenever you take a vacation, collect postcards. There are also people who collect antique postcards that make interesting slide/tape programs.

51. Photocopy comic strips on a copy stand. Cut or white out the conversation balloons of one of the characters. Project the slides and ask students to fill in the missing dialog. This may be used to stimulate oral communication skills or foreign language conversation.

52. A fun rainy day activity is to take colored print photographs of the faces or torsos of each student. Cut out around the image of each student and glue the image to a magazine picture of a celebrity so that it looks as if the student is part of the picture. Copy onto slide form. Project and ask students to explain what they would say to their celebrity.

53. There are many skill-related slide/tape programs that teachers can produce, from how to tie a shoe to how to use a dictionary. Slide/tape programs may be used by the whole class or small groups (in a corner) to review the skill.

54. Have students use modeling clay to sculpture people and animals. Use a close-up lens to take close-up pictures of these figures. Students can use this technique to illustrate a story or happening. They can write a script or narrate the slides. They can make dioramas of legendary figures of, say, colonial life by placing scenic pictures behind the clay figures.

55. Use the copy stand to take 20 or so slides of old movie characters or other subjects. Place them in plastic slide holders that fit into three-ring notebooks (available at photo stores). Distribute these to groups of four or five students. Ask them to arrange the slides into a sequence that tells a story. They must write a script (using production script forms) and make a presentation to the class.

56. Teach the meaning of words by assigning words to students and asking them to find magazine pictures illustrating the meaning of their assigned word. Have them print the word on white paper placed at the bottom of the picture. Copy the pictures and words onto slides. Use to teach or review the meaning of words.

57. Give students pocket cameras and ask them to produce a photo essay on their own life, their hobby, their pets, or family. Require that they storyboard their presentation before taking any slides. They then narrate their story.

58. To teach the appreciation of poetry, ask the class to select a popular song. Play the record and have students write down the lyrics. Have them print the lyrics onto large butcher paper. Photograph the lyrics in a series of slides. Project as the record or tape is played. Point out that the lyric of the song is actually poetry.

59. Assign a concept such as "responsibility" to the class. Let students check out pocket cameras over a period of time. Ask them to take two slides at home illustrating responsibility. They then write a brief explanation about each slide. Slides are put into the slide tray and the explanations read onto tape. Thus you have a slide/tape on responsibility from a student's point of view. Use to discuss concepts such as private property, rights, rules, etc.

60. If you do not have access to cameras, use write-on slides available at camera stores. Have students make simple stick figure drawings or write words on the slides with a felt pen. Small images may also be traced. Use to produce story-type slide/tape programs.

61. School districts sometimes have outdoor education programs in which students spend a day or two at an outdoor campus. Give groups of students film and a camera and ask them to make a photo essay report of their experience out of doors.

62. When studying weather, ask students to take pictures of different cloud formations, rain, hail, thunderstorms, etc. Have them make notes of the TV or newspaper weather report each day corresponding to each slide. Have them write a script on weather using production storyboard forms. They may use their notes on the weather reports for material about each slide. They then produce a slide/tape program on weather.

63. When producing slide/tape programs for discussion, insert black slides in the spots where you want to stop and discuss. Black slides may be made by cutting posterboard the size of cardboard slide mounts with a paper cutter.

64. Take slides of different types of texture such as brick, gravel, silk, sandpaper, corrugated paper, etc. Project the slides and ask students to write descriptive adjectives about each slide. They may use words like *smooth, coarse, slippery, jagged,* and many others. Use to broaden their vocabulary.

65. Take a set of slides depicting line, shape, form, and texture. Place the slides on a light table and ask a task force of three to four students to sort and place each slide in one of the classifications. This may be done to teach a number of discrimination skills.

66. Use the slide projector as an art enlarger. Drawings photographed on the copy stand can be projected onto white or butcher paper taped to the wall. Trace the enlarged projected images onto the paper with felt pens. Use to make classroom maps, murals, banners, posters, and charts.

67. Sometimes community resource people cannot come to your classroom at the desired time. Go out and photograph them in their environment. Have them tell their story onto tape. Match the slides with the narration to form a slide/tape program.

68. Teach visual discrimination skills by photographing several alphabets of captial, lower-case, cursive, and manuscript letters. Use two slide projectors to project two letters at one time. Discuss whether the letters are the same or different.

69. Produce a set of slides with words which are synonyms and antonyms. Students must decide whether the words on each slide are synonyms or antonyms.

70. Photograph the face of a clock with the hands in different positions. Project the slides to drill on the telling of time.

71. Using a saw, cut a sheet of Plexiglas into squares 2 x 2 inches. Scratch, doodle, paint, or draw with pens, pencils, and crayons onto the surface. A great many different effects may be obtained. Project the slides while playing mood music.

72. Use a camera to record the growth of a plant or flower in the classroom. Each day for 36 days take one shot of the plant. Then project the slides in succession and watch the plant grow. Ask students to record their observations and use for discussion.

73. Use photography to study light and how it affects the appearance of an object. Set up a still life in a corner of the classroom near a window. Photograph the still life throughout the day. Project the slides and discuss how our perceptions change as light conditions change.

74. Another rainy day activity is to ask students to bring their baby pictures to you. Copy them onto slides. Project onto the screen and see if students can guess the babies' identities.

75. A fun activity for Christmas is to have several classes participate in writing a Christmas story. The first group storyboards 15 shots of the story. They illustrate and record their part of the story onto tape. This is passed on to the next class which does the same. After three or four classes have completed their section, have an assembly and project the full story.

76. Place a set of slides in a projection tray, with a black slide in every other slot. Project the first slide. Let the students study it for 30 to 40 seconds. Then advance to the black slide. Ask students to describe in detail the slide they have just seen. Back up the projector to check their observations against the slide. Black slides are made by cutting a 2 x 2-inch square out of posterboard with a paper cutter.

77. Ask a student to keep a photographic diary by taking one shot of something important in his life each day. After a 20- or 36-exposure roll has been taken, have him or her make a presentation to the class and answer questions about the experience.

78. Using a copy stand and close-up lenses or the Ektagraphic Visualmaker, a wide variety of map material may be copied into slide form for use in the classroom. Maps should be simple, not too detailed. An 80-slide Carousel tray will hold a wealth of map material in a small space.

79. Use two projectors. On one screen project a geographical feature such as a bay, lake, river bend, or crossroad. On the other screen show how these are symbolized on a map.

80. Photograph the shapes of states. Project quickly to drill class on how to identify states by their shape. You can also use shapes to teach the capitals of each state.

81. Send for photographs of the Earth from NASA and copy onto slide form. Use to teach a number of concepts, such as the continents, or how maps compare to real features photographed from space.

82. Copy weather maps out of the newspapers and use to present and discuss weather and how it changes. Visually compare weather maps for a week to show how storms form.

83. Use dramatized situations to teach bicycle and sidewalk safety in your community. Teach how to cross dangerous streets and how to deal with special hazards.

84. If an art teacher is not available at your school, use a resource person (artist) to present step by step how to make a string drawing, scratchboard, and other projects. Photograph these demonstrations and make into slide/tape programs for use in the future.

85. Teach colors by photographing colors from a paint chip chart (available from paint stores). Visually compare colors or use chips to form a color wheel of primary and secondary colors.

86. Teach children how to react to strangers who offer them rides or candy by dramatizing these situations and photographing them. Use to discuss how children should handle these situations.

87. Use close-up slides of flowers, leaves, tree bark, and grass to teach a nature appreciation unit. Also use to discuss how to identify flowers and trees. Using two projectors, visually compare shapes and colors by projecting two images side by side.

88. As a part of an environmental study, assign students topics to research such as soft and hard waste, water pollution, and toxic chemical disposal in your community or state. Have them research the problem and look for magazine pictures to illustrate their findings. They then write a script, copy the photographs onto slides, and make a slide/tape presentation to your class and other classes.

89. Ask students to research a foreign country. Divide the class into research groups. Let them select from a list a topic to research, such as art, industry, culture, or history. After they have researched the information, students are to locate pictures illustrating their findings. Copy onto slides and have them storyboard a script and produce a slide/tape program. Next year choose another country, and use these presentations as models to help students research other countries. Have students write to embassies, chambers of commerce, and travel bureaus for visual materials.

90. Ask students to bring photographs of their pets. Divide the class into groups having similar pets. Ask them to storyboard a presentation on how to take care of their pet. Loan them instamatic cameras to visualize their report. Use these presentations in class to discuss the care of animals.

91. Ask a professional photographer to come to class and take the students onto the playground for a demonstration of basic photography. Have him demonstrate basic techniques of lighting and composition by posing students and taking shots. After the film is developed, use the slides in class to demonstrate and discuss basic photography.

92. For students having trouble writing the alphabet, buy a sheet of white rub-on letters. Apply them in alphabetical order on sheets of black construction paper. Copy onto slides. Project onto the chalkboard (as white letters). Have students trace the letters to learn the alphabet.

93. For a study on advertising, have students storyboard a commercial to sell a product. Have them film and record the sound track. Use to discuss the propaganda element of commercials.

94. Select a story from a children's audio disc or tape. Ask students to act out the story using hand puppets. Photograph the puppets during the story. Use the slides and disc or tape as a visual presentation. This is a good way to develop special holiday material.

95. Use lettering from a Scrabble game as lettering for slide/tape titles, graphics, and credits. Arrange and photograph.

96. Ask students to take pictures of cool colors or warm colors found in the community. Have them write a script and present the program to the class. Use later to teach the concept of cool and warm colors.

97. Copy a set of cartoon drawings out of *Mad* magazine. Use to illustrate and explain satire.

98. Assign students to watch TV commercials and then develop a storyboard and produce a commercial imitating one of them. Use to announce upcoming school events at back-to-school night, parent conferences, or community service clubs.

99. Ask students to write a story or script about the world as viewed by a pair of shoes. Students then take all the shots from shoe level and read the script onto tape. Use to discuss perspective and our differing viewpoints.

100. Ask students to write a story about the world as viewed by a tree. Students may take shots from a perch in a tree. They can take pictures throughout the school year from the tree. Use to discuss the four seasons and weather.

10
75 Ideas for Using Slides and Slide/Tape Programs in the Secondary School

1. Using old yearbooks as resource material, assign students to produce a slide/tape history of the school.

2. Students often do not understand the function of the city council. Assign a group to attend council meetings, take pictures, and produce a slide/tape program on its function.

3. Have students interview local government officials from the mayor to the county commissioners. Take pictures of the officials being interviewed. Record and edit the interviews into a sound track for a slide/tape program.

4. Assign students to research the local juvenile program in the police department. Have students plan and storyboard the procedure police go through in arresting and booking a teenager who has committed an offense. This can be role played to give a very realistic picture.

5. Take a set of slides of different scenes in the community. As a vocabulary exercise, ask students to write down five words describing what they see. Then ask them to use a thesaurus to locate a synonym for each of the five words.

6. A creative approach to writing is to assign students to produce a slide/tape program of a "snake's eye" view of the world. They have to take all shots from the eye level of a snake. Then they write their perception of the world from this viewpoint and read it onto tape for the sound track.

7. To illustrate how an author creates a character in a story, have students plan and storyboard a fictional character and his thoughts as he views the world — or perhaps the school grounds. Record the script and present to a writing class.

8. To teach a lesson on stereotyping, dress one person or a couple in a number of different types of dress, such as bib overalls, suit and tie, evening gown, etc. Take shots so as to disguise the person(s). Project the slides to the class and have students write their feelings toward each person as portrayed. Record their comments and play back as you show the slides. Then tell them that all pictures were of the same person(s).

9. Have students plan and produce a slide/tape presentation on a "typical day" at your school. Exchange the slide/tape program with a school in another part of the country or in another country. You will have to set this up ahead of time with the other teacher.

10. Have students interview elderly people reminiscing about the community. Record the interviews and take slides of the people being interviewed. Take close-ups of facial expressions. Edit the tape into a sound track for the slide/tape presentation.

11. If you are a drama teacher, take slides of stage scenery and the step-by-step process of making it to show future classes.

12. Take shots of the main characters of a play and their costumes and makeup. Make into a slide/tape presentation to show future students the quality goals you have set for each production.

13. In a geometry class, make assignments practical by photographing real-life problems for students to solve, such as the volume of dirt to be removed on a building project.

14. Have students research environmental problems in your community. Have them plan and produce a slide/tape program on one or more of these problems. Contact service clubs such as Rotary or Lions for permission to present the program at one of their meetings.

15. Use a slide/tape program in an industrial arts class to demonstrate safety procedures while operating equipment. Use several times a year for review.

16. Use a slide/tape program in an industrial arts class to present projects students have done in the past to give current students ideas for projects and the quality you expect.

17. Use a slide/tape presentation to orient students to the function of the school counselor. Present ideas as to how he or she can help students.

18. Use a slide/tape program to give an orientation to the library/media center, where different types of materials are located, and how to use the card catalog or computer to locate them.

19. Produce a slide/tape program presenting the function of library/media specialists and how they can assist students.

20. Produce a slide/tape program on basic research procedures and tools, such as how to use the *Readers' Guide to Periodical Literature* and other reference materials.

21. Produce a slide/tape program on services available at local public libraries. Explain interlibrary loan and computer networks such as OCLC.

22. Produce a slide/tape program on how to handle a research assignment, from choosing the initial topic to producing the final written report. Use to explain what is expected of students in your class.

23. Take pictures of students using the library/media center. Produce a slide/tape program on a day in the center. Show at back-to-school night or to service organizations.

24. Have students interested in photography cover the highlights of the school year, special events, and student achievements. Have them make a slide/tape presentation at a school assembly at the end of the school year.

25. In a psychology class, begin a discussion on good manners today and what is expected of men and women. Assign students to research and produce a slide/tape program on this. Use as a discussion springboard. Not everyone may agree with the group's findings.

26. Use slide/tape programs to teach foreign language conversation. Different social situations can be dramatized, such as a dinnertime, meeting on a street corner, or meeting at a store. The audio would be set up so that one character would be talking to the audience. The audience is asked questions which require a response. Use for vocabulary development and practice in conversation.

27. In an art appreciation class, use two projectors to visually compare the painting styles of two artists. Having two visuals on the screen allows students to discover similarities and differences.

28. Use a slide/tape program to visualize a job interview. Use over-the-shoulder shots to get the viewpoint of the interviewer and the person being interviewed. Dramatize the type of questions that are often asked and good responses.

29. Using high-contrast black-and-white film (available at Kodak camera stores), shoot a number of different types of graphs. Project onto the chalkboard and have students plot the information given in an assignment. You can use this technique for bar or line graphs.

30. Explore occupations by producing a slide/tape program on the life of a person in an occupation—accountant, computer programmer, doctor, etc. Such a program will help students explore occupations in a real-life setting.

31. Using old magazines and newspapers and a copy stand, copy old photographs for a presentation on the history of your community.

32. Have students collect and bring photographs of themselves from infancy. Copy into slide form. Have them write a script to produce a slide/tape autobiography.

33. Have students take shots of a busy shopping center. Encourage them to observe the physical environment and ask them to record the sounds of the location. Using multiple recorders placed in different parts of the classroom, have them recreate the setting and allow the audience members to feel that they were actually there. A multi-screen presentation would be even better.

34. A fun activity is to interview students with a set of questions written out. Photograph the students being interviewed so the class knows who they are. After the interview change the questions and narrate them onto tape. You will have to use reel-to-reel tape. By cutting and splicing, insert the new questions. An original question might be, "Where is your tongue?" and the answer "In my mouth." Insert the question "Where do you keep your gym shoes?"

35. A good, simple way to produce a video program with limited equipment is to produce a slide/tape program, then project it onto a screen and videotape it. This allows you to include out-of-door activities difficult to get without sophisticated video equipment, and editing slides is easier than editing videotape.

36. For a geology class, include with a collection of fossils a slide/tape program visualizing the location and rock formation in which they were found.

37. Take slides of projects made for science or social studies fairs. Use to give students project ideas for next year.

38. Ask students who are doing a research project to photograph it as it progresses. Use slides to document a science experiment. Have students write a script about the process and findings. Present to other classes to demonstrate how a research project is done.

39. Use the free-loan slide/tape programs from Kodak to teach photography or as models for slide/tape production. You may obtain a catalog of free-loan presentations by writing to Kodak, Consumer Markets Division, Rochester, NY 14650.

40. Ask students to produce a slide/tape program of a dream (real or imagined). Use a fog filter on the camera lens to get a dreamy feeling. Students can copy pictures from different sources or take the shots themselves.

41. Use a slide/tape program to clarify values. Have students dramatize a hypothetical situation and ask, "What would you do in this situation?" For example, suppose you found a bag of money containing $50,000. No one but you knows that you found it. Leave the presentations open-ended for oral and written responses.

42. Produce a visual dictionary of word meanings. Give students a list of words and a stack of old magazines and ask them to look for pictures that illustrate the meanings of the assigned words. Write out the words on white paper with a pen. Copy the graphics and pictures into a slide presentation. Use to discuss the meaning of words.

43. Use a slide/tape program in a creative writing class to explore hobbies. Each student is allowed four to five slides to visualize the hobby and writes a brief script (one production storyboard sheet). Have students place their slides in a Carousel tray and in the same order narrate their script onto tape. Use to broaden student awareness of possible hobbies.

44. Photograph on a copy stand the words to songs. Record a piano or instrumental accompaniment. Use for a sing-along or music appreciation class. Make a slide/tape program of a variety of music to broaden student awareness.

45. In a health education class, divide the class into work groups. Assign them to research and produce slide/tape programs on topics in health, such as drugs, smoking, AIDS, and other current problems. The finished programs might be used later by school counselors or nurses.

46. If you are an art teacher, there are many things you can do with slide/tape programs. In lieu of a field trip you can produce a presentation on an art gallery, art show, art displays, art from other countries, and art in the history of man.

47. For an effective presentation on trash pollution in your city, have students take shots of several types of pollution such as junked cars, waste paper, smoking trucks, unauthorized dumping, ugly billboards, faded signs, trash along a river, and smog. Include with a narration, sound effects such as sirens, and appropriate music.

48. Business teachers can use a slide/tape program to present different types of business forms, from order forms to all forms used to follow up an order to the final shipment.

49. A science teacher can use extreme close-ups of insects, cross sections of fruits or nuts, scientific drawings, and charts copied from scientific books or magazines. All these different visual components can be integrated into a slide/tape program.

50. A slide/tape program on table decoration and setting may be produced for home economics. Do's and don't's may be visualized. Ideas may be taken from magazines and books.

51. Use slide/tape programs to explain school bus rules and regulations to parents and students. Illustrate the rules by photographing students on buses.

52. Use high-contrast slides (Kodalith) of words to a song. Project on a screen behind a choral group as they sing. The audience can follow the words and sing along with the group. Divide the song into phrases and project as the group sings those words.

53. Use captioned slides with deaf students to develop word comprehension and vocabulary. These can be made by taking colored prints, adding rub-on lettering and recopying on slide film with a copy stand.

54. Play mood music. Ask students to find pictures in magazines that illustrate their feelings stimulated by the music. Copy the pictures onto slide film and project with the music. Use as a springboard to a creative writing or art assignment.

55. A variation to the above activity is to buy at a photo store a set of write-on slides. Ask students to illustrate their feelings about the music by writing or drawing on the slides with felt-tipped pens. Have them arrange the slides in a sequence and project with the music.

56. For poster, sign, and banner production, copy dry transfer lettering on a copy stand onto slide film. Have students project lettering onto poster board or paper tacked to the wall. They should first make guidelines on the paper, then project the lettering in the proper place. They trace the lettering to produce enlarged lettering.

57. Use a copy stand to copy note cards and examples of outlines and bibliographies to help students understand the correct method for writing a research paper.

58. Use two slide projectors together to project visual contrasts or comparisons — for example, two pieces of pottery from different eras or cultures.

59. Use three projectors together to visualize an object such as a sculpture from three different angles. For example, you may use a medium shot, close-up, and extreme close-up, or varied angle shots. Have students study the shots and write down their observations.

60. In a geology class use two or three projectors to visualize a rock formation on one screen and close-ups of rocks found in the formation on the other screen.

61. Produce a slide/tape program visualizing the procedures you require in your classroom. Pose students at the pencil sharpener, passing in papers, etc., to visualize these procedures.

62. Take shots of dioramas, displays, and exhibits in a museum. Use to produce a slide/tape program on local history or use individually with a class lecture.

63. Assign students to conduct an opinion poll of prominent citizens in the community. Have students record the citizens' comments and photograph them. Organize into a slide/tape program on the pros and cons of a key issue.

64. Use a copy stand to take slides of magazine and newspaper pictures of state and national political figures. Use to discuss election issues or the function of government or to help students identify those in public office.

65. Use a microcomputer and colored monitor to produce graphics, titles, and graphs for a slide program. Photograph using a telephoto lens.

66. Use a slide/tape program to introduce students to a new make or model of microcomputer. Visualize how to operate it and how it differs from previous models.

67. Use a slide/tape program to visualize how to operate a new computer software program. Use as a training tool before hands-on computer operation.

68. Assign a class to research how different businesses and companies are using microcomputers. Have students take shots of computer applications and produce a slide/tape program. Use as an introduction to a computer class.

69. In a math class, write out theorems and equations on paper. Use a copy stand to copy onto slides. Use as a quick review at the beginning of a class.

70. Use a slide/tape program to present phone etiquette.

71. In home economics, use a slide/tape program to produce a visual recipe. Visualize step by step how bread or a cake is baked following the recipe.

72. In home economics visualize how a cake decorator is used and ideas for cake decoration.

73. In home economics, visualize types of salads, snack tray arrangement, and appetizers. Many of these ideas can be copied from magazines using a copy stand.

74. In home economics visualize ideas for table centerpieces, table decorations, and holiday decoration ideas.

75. If your classroom doesn't have room darkening, make a rear projection screen out of a cardboard box. Cut a 2 x 3 ratio rectangle out of the bottom of the box. Use frosted acetate or translucent paper as a screen. Project from behind the screen. If slides have captions, reverse them in the tray so that they won't be backward on the screen.

11

26 Ideas for Using Slides and Slide/Tape Programs in Public Relations

1. Slide/tape programs work well to visualize the need for new or remodeled school facilities and the passage of a bond issue. Use at parent groups or community service groups.

2. Develop a computer-scored response sheet for use with a presentation on the need for a bond issue. People can give opinions and respond anonymously. This can give you feedback for revising your presentation or changing the emphasis.

3. Use a slide/tape program to visualize the goals of your school district or organization. Use to orient your employees to the goals and the part they play in attaining them.

4. Visualize administrative structure by photographing an organizational chart and the people represented. Use to inform the public and employees about the job each person in the organization performs.

5. Produce a visualized history of a school, district, community, or organization. Use a copy stand to photograph old newspapers, photo albums, annuals, and other historic documents. Often service organizations, libraries, and civic organizations are looking for programs like this.

6. Use a slide/tape program to illustrate what to do in a disaster. Use volunteers to demonstrate the correct procedures and photograph them. Use for civic and service organization programs.

7. Develop community career awareness by producing a slide/tape program on careers in the community. Photograph people being interviewed on the job. Use to help students become aware of career opportunities in your community.

8. Use a slide/tape program to initiate a United Way drive. Visualize the goals and how the money is distributed. Present to employees of large companies, service organizations, etc.

9. Present the services offered by the school or public library using a slide/tape program.

10. Ask someone not connected with your school or organization to take shots of your organization from the viewpoint of a visitor. Use the slides to discuss how to improve the image presented by the building and organization.

11. Photograph parents or community leaders speaking of the value of your organization or program. Use as a PR tool to promote your program in the community.

12. Shoot a slide/tape program on a day with a student, employee, or city official. Use to inform audiences of the tasks, problems, or activities faced by that person. The community may not have any perception of the difficulties and problems faced by a student, teacher, employee, or city council member.

13. Use a slide/tape program to develop awareness of trash pollution. Set up scenes of different types of trash pollution and shoot each one separately. Demonstrate the proper way to dispose of trash.

14. Take shots of floats in city parades. Use slides to give your organization ideas for designing a float for the next parade.

15. Slide/tape programs are powerful tools to change attitudes. Use them to change public opinion about an issue you feel strongly about. Photograph influential citizens and record their arguments as part of the program. Show to civic, service, and parent organizations.

16. Use a slide/tape program to visualize the type of community services available to citizens, such as swimming, exercise, seminars, courses, and sports facilities. Present to service clubs.

17. Use a slide/tape program to visualize a demographic study of a community and its growth in the next 15 years. Use to make people aware of actions needed now to insure the quality of life desired in the future.

18. An effective way to shock people into awareness of pollution is to take a song such as "This Is My Country" and accompany the first verse with beautiful scenic slides. On the second verse, project ugly scenes with all types of pollution. Use a copy stand and magazine pictures or take shots of the community.

19. Choose a "citizen of the year," someone who has done exceptional community service. Use a copy stand to make slides of colored prints of their family, pets, and hobbies. Take posed shots of them doing community service. Honor this person by presenting this program at community day celebrations, banquets, and civic meetings.

20. At the end of a slide/tape program include a graphic slide listing questions for discussion or problems to be solved. Leave the slide on the screen and use as a focus point for a discussion or buzz session by the audience.

21. If you own a company or are a personnel manager hiring new employees, produce a slide/tape program visualizing benefits other than wages that employees have when they work for your company. Also visualize qualities you seek in a worker.

22. Produce a slide/tape program on how homeowners can better protect their home and possessions from intruders. Deal with a number of home security methods. Offer to give the presentation to clubs and civic groups.

23. If you are teaching art or craft workshops or classes in the community, promote the arts by taking slides of student work, art fairs, or art exhibits.

24. Produce a slide/tape presentation of ideas for community service for retired people. This may be produced by a hospital or organization seeking volunteers. Present to retirement and civic groups.

25. Produce a slide/tape tour of your company or organization. Present the types of services you provide to the community and how individuals may avail themselves of these services. Show at fairs, in shopping malls, and at community day celebrations. Set up a booth with a rear projection screen.

26. Start a business by offering to photograph the furnishings and equipment of a business or residence to establish proof for insurance claims in case of a disaster.

Glossary

ASA — A rating indicating the sensitivity of a film to light, set by the American Standards Association. The ASA doubles as the sensitivity of the film doubles. Replaced by ISO designation.

Bellows — A flexible, light-tight accordian-fold mechanism for 35mm cameras which extends the lens farther from the film plane than normal, for extreme close-up photography.

Cassette tape — A self-contained reel-to-reel one-eighth-inch-wide audio tape installed in a plastic case.

Close-up — A photo in which the camera is focused on the subject or a part of it, eliminating everything else from view.

Colored adhesive — A translucent, thin sheet of adhesive-backed, colored acetate used to add solid, even areas of color to an illustration.

Continuity — The logical progression of photographic images and narration, smoothly flowing from one action to the next.

Copy stand — A stand used to hold a camera in position to photograph printed materials, artwork, or other photographic images.

Credit slide — A slide listing those who assisted or cooperated in the production of a slide/tape program.

Depth of field — The distance within a scene, from the point closest to the camera to the farthest, that is acceptably sharp in the focused image.

Dissolve — The superimposition of two images, or the gradual fading of one image and appearance of a second.

Dissolve unit   A unit having a mechanism for slowing turning one projector off, causing one slide to fade, while another image slowly appears on the same screen, allowing a gradual overlapping, fading, and changing from one visual to another.

Double burn   The double exposing of two slides onto one. One slide may be a scene and the other a high-contrast graphic. This permits the adding of lettering to a scenic slide.

Establishment shot   A long or medium shot which orients the audience to the whereabouts of a sequence of close-up action shots.

Extension tubes   Metal rings which are attached between the lens and the camera body for close-up photography. This permits the lens to be focused closer than normal to an object.

f-stop   The diaphragm setting on a lens, representing the amount of light passing through the lens. The higher the f-stop number, the smaller the lens opening.

Focal length   A method of classifying lens length (in millimeters) as measured from the center of the lens to the film plane.

High-angle shot   A shot taken from a high angle, with the camera placed so as to shoot down on the subject.

High-contrast film (Slides)   Lithography film, usually used in offset printing, used in a 35mm camera. This film does not photograph grays. By photographing black lettering a negative slide is produced and will appear as white lettering on a black background.

ISO   A film speed rating replacing ASA (an abbreviation of International Standards Organization).

Macro lens   A lens designed to take extreme close-up pictures.

Multi-image projection   The simultaneous projection of two or more images on adjacent screens.

Programmer   A unit which can control one or more projectors to change slides according to the timing and sequence specified by a script.

Rear screen projection   Projection onto the back side of a translucent screen.

Release form   A signed form giving a producer permission to use shots of people or their copyrighted materials.

Script	A written planned sequenced of shots with companion narration, music, and graphics.
Sequence	A succession of related shots (pictures) which is more or less a unit, complete in itself.
Shot	Each separate picture (slide) which is the basic element of a slide/tape program.
Single lens reflex camera	A camera using a prism viewing system so that the user can see through the camera lens to compose the picture.
Storyboard	A system for planning each picture in a slide/tape program through the use of verbal description or drawings — a planning tool leading to a more formal written script.
Telephoto lens	A lens that produces a closer view of a subject than could be gotten with a normal lens from the same spot. It magnifies the image much like binoculars.
Treatment	A brief written description of how the content of a slide/tape program will be presented.
Wide-angle lens	A lens designed to give a wider view of the subject than would be obtained by a normal lens from the same spot. An example would be a 28mm lens.
Zoom lens	A lens adjustable to various focal lengths. For example, it allows a quick change from a wide-angle to a telephoto shot.

Appendix A:
Forms and Schedules

SLIDE/TAPE PLANNING SCHEDULE

_____ Select a topic. Keep it *simple* and *narrow*.

_____ Analyze your audience, their background and needs.

_____ Write your objectives. What do you want the audience to do or feel as a result of viewing your presentation?

_____ Write a brief treatment of your presentation. Limit it to a paragraph or two. Describe your program as the audience will see it.

_____ Brainstorm all the possible ideas pertaining to your topic. Write them down. Do not evaluate them yet.

_____ Select key ideas. Eliminate bad ones.

_____ Arrange the key ideas into a sequence. These are the main points of your outline. Add subpoints to flesh out the outline.

_____ Develop a storyboard, using a production script or cards.

_____ Read your storyboard to a friend. Ask for constructive criticism and revise storyboard.

_____ Make a list of shots to be taken, by location. List graphics to be produced. Determine what equipment will be needed.

_____ Take the slides following the shooting list. Be sure to shoot alternate shots, or bracket shoot if unsure of correct exposure.

_____ Produce graphics and shoot them on a copy stand.

_____ Send film to be developed—not to a discount developer.

_____ Select the music and narrator for your presentation.

_____ When developed slides return, *throw away bad ones*. Select and arrange slides following the storyboard.

_____ Revise script or reshoot bad slides.

_____ Type out a professional reading script.

_____ Make a trial presentation, projecting the slides and reading the script. Have several friends critique it. Revise as necessary.

_____ Produce the sound track. Make at least two copies of the tape.

_____ Practice presenting the program until you are comfortable giving it. Ask several individuals at the first audience to give you constructive criticism. You may want to revise again.

_____ When you go out to make your presentation, don't forget to take extension cords, three-pronged adapters, spare projection lamps, a flashlight, and other accessories.

TOPIC AND OBJECTIVES WORKSHEET

Possible presentation topic _____

_____

Remember to keep the topic narrow and simple. You must be able to cover your topic adequately with 80 slides (single projector) or 160 slides (dissolve unit with 2 projectors) or use 140-slide trays. However, for instructional purposes limit a program to 20-25 minutes; for lower elementary, 10-11 minutes.

Write a brief description (treatment) of your presentation. Describe it as the audience will see it.

Analyze your target audience as to age, profession, special interests, and educational background.

Write three to five specific objectives. State objectives in terms of specific behaviors you want the audience to evidence as a result of viewing your presentation. In the skill area, they should be able to perform the skill or practice it as a result of viewing the program. You may want to specify the level of acceptable performance, such as "Viewers should be able to list three of the five characteristics presented." Avoid vague words such as *appreciate, understand,* and *know.* These are impossible to measure. Study the list of words for objectives in the following section.

Write out three to five objectives below.

1.

2.

3.

4.

5.

Words Suitable for Objectives

Cognitive Behavior

Lower-level Tasks

formulate	attend	collect	complete	diagram	document
copy	count	define	describe	find	include
designate	detect	distinguish	distribute	cite	circle
duplicate	find	identify	differentiate	classify	compile
imitate	indicate	isolate	discriminate	arrange	attempt
label	list	mark	name	categorize	chart
note	match	omit	order	tally	tell
place	point to	provide	recall	underline	volunteer
repeat	select	sort	state		

Analysis Tasks

analyze	appraise	combine	compare	structure	save
conclude	contrast	criticize	deduce	switch	shorten
defend	evaluate	explain	formulate	plan	
generate	induce	infer	paraphrase	present	

Synthesis Tasks

alter	change	design	discover	expand	generalize
extend	modify	regroup	rename	rearrange	recombine
reorder	restate	retell	rewrite	restructure	
signify	simplify	synthesize	systematize	reconstruct	

Affective Behavior (Attitudinal)

accept	agree	allow	answer	buy	help
excuse	forgive	interact	cooperate	join	compliment
laugh	lend	meet	praise	offer	volunteer
serve	shape	smile	talk	thank	disagree
participate	communicate				

Psychomotor Behavior

manipulate	operate	clean	fix	pull apart	demonstrate

Words That Are Difficult to Measure and Are to Be Avoided

believe	experience	feel	hear	know	listen
perceive	realize	see	think	feeling	enjoyment
recognize	understand	awareness	attitude	interest in	appreciate
understanding		knowledge of			

STORYBOARD SCRIPT

Page _____ of _____

TITLE: _____

BASIC READING SCRIPT FORM
WITH INSTRUCTIONS

VISUAL INSTRUCTIONS	SLIDE NUMBER	AUDIO
VISUAL INSTRUCTIONS GO DIRECTLY OPPOSITE AUDIO INSTRUCTIONS AT THE PRECISE POINT AT WHICH SOMETHING SHOULD OCCUR	1	SPECIFIC AUDIO INSTRUCTIONS SUCH AS <u>FADE IN MUSIC . . . FADE UNDER NARRATION</u> . . . ARE WRITTEN IN CAPITALS AND UNDERLINED. When writing scripts, put all visual descriptions on the left and all audio on the right. Double space all audio copy. Keep even margins on the left. Never break a word at the end of a line, nor a sentence at the end of a page.
VISUAL INSTRUCTIONS GO ON THE LEFT IN CAPS AND ARE SINGLE-SPACED IF MORE THAN ONE LINE IS REQUIRED FOR ONE SET OF INSTRUCTIONS	2	To indicate emphasis in a script, underline words to be stressed. Also, underline all information that refers to music or sound other than the actual words to be read. <u>THESE DIRECTIONS ARE UNDERLINED AND ARE IN ALL CAPITALS.</u>
FOR SLIDE SCRIPTS, PUT THE NUMBER OF THE SLIDE IN THE MIDDLE BETWEEN THE AUDIO AND THE VISUAL COLUMNS AND AT THE EXACT POINT YOU WANT TO SEE THAT SLIDE.	3	Write out the words the way you want them to be expressed (for example, "three dollars and eighty cents" vs. "three-eighty").
DESCRIPTIONS OF SLIDES SHOULD BE CONCISE BUT EXACT. THEY SHOULD INCLUDE TYPE OF SHOT (CU, ECU, MS, LA, ETC.)	4	Each page of a multiple-page script, except for the first one, should be numbered at the top. Write "MORE" at the bottom center of each page except the last one.

MORE

SLIDE DESCRIPTIONS CAN ALSO BE SIMPLE DRAWINGS. THESE ARE GOOD FOR GRAPHICS, CHARTS, PICTOGRAMS, OR SPECIAL EFFECTS.

5   If the script is a partial script, be sure to include the outcue. For example, a script may have long stretches without narration. An outcue will cue slide changes.

SLIDE DESCRIPTIONS CAN ALSO BE SIMPLE DRAWINGS SUCH AS STICK FIGURES.

6   Make sure all of the above instructions are adhered to on the script. Remember, others working with you will be counting on it.

Special Tips for Scripting

1. Choose words carefully. Don't use more than you need. Think of words costing 25 cents each, as in a telegram.

2. Write in conversational tone. Read the script out loud to confirm that it reads well, or have someone read it to you.

3. Vary your shots. Use high- and low-angle shots rather than having them all eye level. Photograph pets and children from their eye level.

4. Use medium and close-up shots to tell the story. Too often slides become a series of snapshots and lack visual impact.

5. Remember you are developing an *audiovisual* program. Try to visualize the situations you are describing. Reorient yourself to think in pictures. The visuals will carry at least 80 percent of the message.

6. The narration is important not only for the part it plays in explaining details as the *audio* of "audiovisual"; it also may call attention to relationships and indicate emphasis that should be given in some pictures. Avoid describing what the audience sees on the screen.

SAMPLE SHOOTING ASSIGNMENT FORM

GRAPHICS TO BE PRODUCED

1. Title slide	7.
2. Credit slide	8.
3. Ending slide	9.
4.	10.
5.	11.
6.	12.

OUTDOOR SHOTS BY LOCATION

Location:

Location:

Location:

Location:

INDOOR SHOTS BY LOCATION

Location:

Location:

Location:

Location:

EXAMPLE OF A MODEL RELEASE FORM

MODEL RELEASE

Date _____

Photographer _____

Street _____ City _____ State _____

Zip _____ Phone ( ) _____

For valuable consideration, I hereby irrevocably consent to and authorize the use and reproduction by you, or anyone authorized by you, of any and all photographs which you have this day taken of me, negative or positive, proofs of which are hereto attached, for any purpose whatsoever, without further compensation to me. All negatives and positives, together with the prints, shall constitute your property, solely and completely.

I am over 18 years of age.   Yes _____   No _____

MODEL _____
Signature of Model

Address _____

Phone ( ) _____

Witnessed by: _____
Signature of Witness or Notary

* * * * * * * *

If the person signing is under 18, consent should be given by parent or guardian, as follows:

I hereby certify that I am the parent or guardian of

_____

the model named above, and for value received I do give my consent without reservations to the foregoing on behalf of him or her or them.

Dated: _____

Witnessed by: _____
Signature of Witness or Notary

MASK FOR 35mm SLIDES

This is an outline of a mask for making 35mm slides on the copy stand. Its area, 6 x 9 inches, fits the required 2:3 aspect ratio. *Never* design artwork on a vertical format. All graphics should be *horizontal.* Vertical slides bleed off of rectangular screens.

SAMPLE SLIDE/TAPE PRESENTATION
EVALUATION FORM

Title of presentation _____

Name of presenter _____

Who is the target audience? _____

GRAPHIC SLIDES:

Title shot _____ excellent _____ good _____ needs work _____ poor

Credit slide(s) _____ excellent _____ good _____ need work _____ poor

Charts _____ excellent _____ good _____ need work _____ poor

Maps _____ excellent _____ good _____ need work _____ poor

Word graphics _____ excellent _____ good _____ need work _____ poor

Illustrations _____ excellent _____ good _____ need work _____ poor

Other:

PICTURE QUALITY:

Exposure _____ excellent _____ some overexposed _____ some underexposed

Composition _____ excellent _____ needs work _____ poor

Shots _____ tell story well _____ lack close-ups
_____ lack variety of shots _____ lack visual impact

Pictorial Continuity _____ good _____ needs work _____ poor

SCRIPT:

_____ flows well _____ pace good _____ pace too slow
_____ pace too fast _____ too wordy _____ narration drags
_____ narration too long per slide _____ describes objects on screen

(continues on next page)

ACCURACY OF INFORMATION:

_____ very good   _____ fair   _____ inaccurate; needs work

SOUND TRACK:

_____ tape quality good   _____ tape quality poor
_____ narration enunciation clear   _____ narration enunciation poor
_____ volume good   _____ volume too low   _____ volume too high
_____ music ties in with mood   _____ music inappropriate
other _____

Appendix B:
Materials and Services

FREE-LOAN SLIDE/TAPE PROGRAMS ON PHOTOGRAPHY

For a catalog of slide/tape programs on photography write to:
Eastman Kodak Company
Dept. 454
343 State Street
Rochester, NY 14651

GRAPHIC ARTS SUPPLIES

The following companies market a large number of graphic arts materials such as dry transfer lettering, colored tapes from 1/64th to one inch for graphs, decorative border tapes, symbols and texture films, colored film to add large solid areas of color, and colored paper for slide graphic backgrounds.

Chartpak
Customer Service Dept.
One River Road
Leeds, MA 01053

Letraset Inc.
2379 Charleston Road
Mt. View, CA 94040

Artype Inc.
345 East Terra Cotta Ave.
Crystal Lake, IL 60014

Prestype Corp.
194 Veterans Boulevard
Carlstadt, NH 07072

PLASTIC LETTERING GUIDES

Wrico Lettering Guides
Warren-Knight Instrument Co.
2000 Bennett Road
Philadelphia, PA 19116

Clip Art Illustrations

A. A. Archibold Publishers
P. O. Box 57985
Los Angeles, CA 09957

Harry Volk Art Studio
Pleasantville, NJ 08232

Gummed-Back Die-Cut Letters

Democo
Box 1488
Madison, WI 53701

Stik-a-Letter Co.
Route 2, Box 1400
Escondido, CA 90027

Programmers and Dissolve Units

AVL
500 Hillside Ave.
Atlantic Highlands, NJ 07716

ARION Corporation
825 Boone Ave. North
Minneapolis, MN 55427

Eastman Kodak Company
Ektagraphic Dissolve Unit
343 State St.
Rochester, NY 14650

Clear Light
Cornerstone Associates, Inc.
123 Second Ave.
Waltham, MA 02154

Bibliography

SLIDE/TAPE PRODUCTION

Adventures in Color Slide Photography. Rochester, N.Y.: Eastman Kodak Company, 1976.

Gordon, Roger L., ed. *The Art of Multi-Image.* Washington, D.C.: Association for Multi-Image, 1978.

Images, Images, Images. Rochester, N.Y.: Eastman Kodak Company, 1979.

Kemp, Jerrold E. *Planning and Producing Audiovisual Materials,* 4th ed. New York: Harper and Row, 1980.

League of Women Voters. *Project Your Image: How to Produce a Slide Show,* publication no. 296. Washington, D.C.: League of Women Voters of the United States, 1977.

Lee, Robert, and Robert Misiorowski. *Script Models, A Handbook for the Media Writer.* New York: Hastings House Publishers, 1978.

Planning and Producing Slide Programs. Rochester, N.Y.: Eastman Kodak Company, 1975.

Producing Slides and Filmstrips. Rochester, N.Y.: Eastman Kodak Company, 1970.

Slides with a Purpose. Rochester, N.Y.: Eastman Kodak Company, 1981.

Sunier, John. *Slide/Sound and Filmstrip Production.* New York: Focal Press, 1981.

Swain, Dwight V. *Film Scriptwriting, A Practical Manual.* London: Focal Press, 1982.

PHOTOGRAPHY AND SLIDE/TAPE PROGRAMS

Your local camera store is one of the best sources of reference materials on photography. Several companies specialize in how-to books on all aspects of photography. Most of these books may be purchased at local camera stores or ordered by them from the publishers. Here are some very helpful books, listed by company:

Eastman Kodak, Motion Picture and Audiovisual Markets Division, Rochester, NY 14650

Adventures in Existing Light, catalog #144-9461

The Art of Seeing, catalog #KW-20

Close-up Photography, The Kodak Workshop Series

Existing Light Photography, The Kodak Workshop Series

The Joy of Photographing People, by The Editors of Eastman Kodak, Addison-Wesley Publishing, 1983

Kodak Films, Color and B & W, catalog #102-6061

Lenses for 35mm Cameras, catalog #144-1757

More Joy of Photography—100 Techniques for More Creative Photographs, by The Editors of Eastman Kodak, Addison-Wesley Publishing, 1981

Photographing with Automatic Cameras

Photographing Your Baby, by The Editors of Eastman Kodak, Addison-Wesley Publishing, 1984

H P Books, P.O. Box 5367, Tuscon, AZ 85703

Camera manuals:
Canon
Medium-Format Cameras
Minolta
Nikon
Olympus
Pentax

How to Compose Better Photos, 1981

How to Control and Use Photographic Lighting, 1980

How to Create Photographic Special Effects, 1979

How to Improve Your Photography, 1981

How to Photograph Sports and Action, 1982

How to Select and Use Electronic Flash, 1983

How to Take Better Travel Photos, 1979

How to Take Pictures Like a Pro, 1982

How to Use Light Creatively, 1981

Pro Techniques of People Photography, 1984

Understanding Photography, 1974

Minolta Corporation Series published by Doubleday and Co., Garden City, NY

Color Photography with Self-teaching Technique Tips, 1982

Flash Photography, 1982

How to Use Filters, 1982

How to Use Your 35mm Camera, 1982

A Modern Photo Guide, Portrait Photography with Self-teaching Technique Tips, 1982

What Lenses Can Do, 1982

Index